Praise for The Power to Change

"Congrats on creating something that will make the world a better place!"
Sharon Lebell, bestselling author of *The Art of Living*

The Power to Change is a gift to anyone seeking to live a more fulfilling life. This book offers a clear and accessible guide to applying Stoic principles in daily life, including practical advice on overcoming obstacles and finding joy in everyday moments. Chakrapani's insights are both enlightening and actionable, making this book a must-read for anyone seeking to transform their life through Stoic philosophy."
Donald J. Robertson, bestselling author of *How to Think Like a Roman Emperor*

"Chakrapani distils ancient Stoic wisdom into practical, actionable guidance for modern life. With clarity and accessibility, he shows how timeless principles can help us overcome overthinking, anxiety, and the constant need for approval. A thoughtful introduction for anyone seeking more tranquility and purpose in today's hectic world."
Massimo Pigliucci, K.D. Irani Professor of Philosophy at the
City College of New York

The Power to Change is an engaging, enthusiastic, and innovative guide to living a good life. Dr Chakrapani masterfully illuminates the power of Stoic wisdom in this lively and compelling book. The practical exercises in each chapter encourage a deeper understanding of the radiant wisdom of the Stoics and offer a clear and practical path to the power to change your life. You don't just read this book; you live this book."
Karen Duffy, NY Times bestselling author of *Model Patient, Backbone* and *Wise Up*

"Chuck Chakrapani has done excellent work in recent years in bringing out the benefits of Stoic life-guidance, for instance, in his insightful monthly journal, THE STOIC. *The Power to Change* offers a wise, thoughtful, but also lively and accessible, manual for transforming your life for the better on Stoic principles. The book is clearly organised to lead you through the process of self-transformation, with perceptive suggestions at each stage."
Christopher Gill, Emeritus Professor of Ancient Thought, University of Exeter,
and founding member of Modern Stoicism; co-author of
Stoic Ethics: the Basics (2025), with Brittany Polat

"Written in a wonderfully concise, direct, and breezy style, this book offers simple, straightforward, yet powerful lessons in good mental hygiene and canny self-improvement. Here we have clear, easy to grasp directions for how not to construct obstacles to a life of smooth, faultless contentment. Chuck's tireless, ongoing work spreading Stoic wisdom deserves much gratitude."

William O. Stephens, Professor Emeritus of Philosophy, Creighton University

"Chuck Chakrapani is one of my favourite modern Stoics. Chuck has the happy knack of making things as simple as they need to be, but no simpler. I would thoroughly recommend this book to anyone wishing to deepen their practice of Stoicism. I particularly appreciated Chuck's engaging style, relevant Stoic quotations and useful exercises. Read it and find out more about the four backseat drivers that we are up against, and how to overcome everyday problems using powerful Stoic ideas."

Tim LeBon, accredited CBT therapist working in the NHS, Research Director of Modern Stoicism and author of *365 Ways to be more Stoic*

"Dr. Chakrapani has written a highly accessible book on implementing Stoicism in today's world. Chuck, a great example of a modern Stoic, is passionate about helping people use Stoic philosophy to face their strongest temptations and significant challenges. He guides people in the practice of the powerful principles of Stoic philosophy. He gently reminds people that consistent practice is challenging but not impossible and well worth the effort. The value of this book is that it accurately informs people of the core ideas of Stoicism and shows them how to implement these ideas in a world encouraging self-defeating indulgence and other short-term, palliative solutions to anxiety and despair. If you want to take control of your emotional reactions to life's burdens and challenges, open your mind to the powerful ideas in this book. By embracing the ideas and strategies presented in this accessible book, readers will be shown how to empower themselves to change what they can and to make peace with what they cannot change."

Walter J. Matweychuk, Ph.D. Psychologist at the University of Pennsylvania Department of Psychiatry; REBTDoctor.com

"Dr. Chuck Chakrapani—one of the preeminent scholar-teachers of modern Stoicism—has written a book for the ages. The purpose of this book, Dr. Chakrapani states, '…is to identify a few simple principles that will create a successful life and provide a clear road map and directions to get there.' *The Power to Change* succeeds admirably in these goals. Among the key Stoic principles, perhaps the central one is, as Chakrapani puts it, 'Some things in life are within your control. Others are not. Ignore what is not within your control and consistently act on what is.' Indeed, in my experience as a psychiatrist, ignoring this principle usually puts one on the psychological road to ruin. Importantly, Chakrapani emphasizes the importance of constant practice in implementing the principles of Stoicism. Throughout this practical, down-to-earth guide to 'the flourishing life,' the author writes in a clear and inviting style, often with a light touch. I believe Dr. Chakrapani's book will serve as an invaluable guide to changing our lives for the better."

Ronald W. Pies, M.D. Professor Emeritus of Psychiatry and Lecturer on Bioethics & Humanities, SUNY Upstate Medical University; Author of *Everything Has Two Handles, The Stoic's Guide to the Art of Living,* and *The Anatomy of Gratitude*

THE POWER TO CHANGE

STOIC STRATEGIES TO
TRANSFORM YOUR LIFE

Chuck Chakrapani

First published in Great Britain by John Murray Business in 2025
An imprint of John Murray Press

1

Copyright © Chuck Chakrapani 2025

The right of Chuck Chakrapani to be identified as the Author of the Work has been
asserted by him in accordance with the Copyright, Designs and Patents Act 1988.

A CIP catalogue record for this title is available from the British Library

Hardback ISBN 978 1 399 82599 3
ebook ISBN 978 1 399 82600 6

Typeset by KnowledgeWorks Global Ltd.

Printed and bound in Great Britain by Clays Ltd, Elcograf S.p.A.

John Murray Press policy is to use papers that are natural, renewable and recyclable
products and made from wood grown in sustainable forests. The logging and
manufacturing processes are expected to conform to the environmental regulations of the
country of origin.

John Murray Press   John Murray Business
Carmelite House   123 S. Broad St., Ste 2750
50 Victoria Embankment   Philadelphia, PA 19109
London EC4Y 0DZ

https://johnmurraybusiness.com/

John Murray Press, part of Hodder & Stoughton Limited
An Hachette UK company

The authorized representative in the EEA is Hachette Ireland, 8 Castlecourt Centre,
Dublin 15, D15 XTP3, Ireland (email: info@hbgi.ie)

To Hita and Raghu

'If you will listen to me, whoever you are, and whatever you are doing, you will not feel suffering or anger, or compulsion, or hindrance. You will pass your time without worries.'

—*EPICTETUS*

CONTENTS

ABOUT THE AUTHOR

From the boardroom to the classroom, Dr. Chuck Chakrapani has consistently sought to understand and improve how we live and work. His career has spanned the highest levels of business leadership, serving as CEO of Millward Brown Canada and President of Leger Analytics and advising Fortune 500 companies, governments, and nonprofits across various industries. Simultaneously, he has pursued a distinguished academic career, holding appointments at institutions like the London Business School and currently serving as Distinguished Visiting Professor at the Ted Rogers School of Management, Toronto Metropolitan University. A renowned data scientist and expert witness, Dr. Chakrapani's expertise is grounded in rigorous analysis and a deep understanding of human behavior.

His prolific writing career reflects this diverse experience. Dr. Chakrapani has authored numerous influential books, from business analytics and financial management to market research. More recently, he has turned his attention to the ancient philosophy of Stoicism, offering a modern and practical lens through which to explore its enduring wisdom. Beginning with *Unshakable Freedom* and the monthly digital magazine *THE STOIC*, he has authored a growing library of books on the subject. He also founded the Prokopton community, a program designed to guide individuals in developing a Stoic practice that cultivates resilience, purpose, and a life of meaning and flow.

Explore Dr. Chakrapani's work on Stoicism at:

https://thestoicgym.substack.com.

INTRODUCTION

Toward a life that flows well

Simple principles can yield profound results. Consider these deceptively simple examples:

Q. What is the essence of the Torah?

A. "What's hateful to you, do not do to others"—Hillel

Q. How do you make money in the stock market?

A. "Buy low, sell high."—conventional wisdom

Q. What is the essence of eating well?

A. "Eat food. Not too much. Mostly plants"—Michael Pollan

While these principles are easy to grasp, we often underestimate their power.

Understanding a principle is merely the first step. It's akin to knowing the destination: "Destination X is 50 miles southwest." This information is useful, but insufficient. We also need a map, directions, and perhaps even a guide to navigate the terrain effectively.

Similarly, knowing a principle requires a roadmap for implementation. We need to translate that knowledge into consistent action. This book aims to identify a few simple, yet powerful, Stoic principles and provide a clear roadmap for applying them to your life. It will guide you in designing a life that flows smoothly and equip you to navigate the challenges you encounter.

These Stoic principles, forged over two millennia, are not only simple but also remarkably robust. They have formed the foundation of many modern psychotherapies, such as cognitive behavioral therapy (CBT) and rational emotive behavior therapy (REBT), demonstrating their enduring relevance and compatibility with contemporary psychological thought.

This book is divided into four parts:

- Part 1 explores the core Stoic principles and their potential for transformative change.
- Part 2 addresses common obstacles that may hinder the implementation of these principles.
- Part 3 guides you in designing a life that flows smoothly and harmoniously.
- Part 4 provides practical strategies for navigating and overcoming everyday challenges.

While these principles are easy to grasp, consistent application is crucial. The greatest rewards will accrue to those who diligently practice these principles and persevere through inevitable plateaus. No amount of knowledge can replace consistent action.

Chuck Chakrapani

PART 1
WHERE ARE WE HEADED?

In Part 1, we embark on our journey toward a good life by exploring some of the core principles identified by the Stoics. These principles are deceptively simple, yet incredibly powerful. By applying them consistently to your life and work, you can experience immediate benefits:

- **Focus on what you can control:** Distinguish between what is within your control and what is not. Concentrate your efforts on what you can influence and let go of what lies beyond your control. Consistent application of this principle will significantly reduce anxiety and worry.

- **Live in the present:** Avoid dwelling on the past or anxiously anticipating the future. By focusing your attention on the present moment, you can cultivate tranquility and inner peace.

- **Recognize the power of your perceptions:** Understand that much of what you experience as "reality" is shaped by your own interpretations and judgments.

- **Act virtuously without delay:** Do not postpone acts of kindness, courage, or justice. Virtuous actions not only benefit others but also contribute to your own personal growth.

- **Focus on what you can control:** Your actions have the greatest impact when you concentrate your efforts on what is within your control.

- **Let go of "if only" thinking:** Dwelling on past regrets or "what ifs" hinders your ability to live fully in the present.

- **Seize the day:** Embrace the present moment and live each day to the fullest, recognizing that time is precious and fleeting.

In the following chapters, we will delve deeper into these profound principles and explore how they can transform your life.

While grasping these principles is relatively easy, consistent practice is essential. I have made every effort to present these principles in a clear and concise manner, and to provide practical guidance for their implementation. Remember, consistent application, not just intellectual understanding, is the key to unlocking the transformative power of these principles.

60 seconds to a happy life

The next 60 seconds can change your life

We can be free, happy, and serene, no matter what else is happening around us, if we understand one basic truth: some things in life are under our control, and others are not. Yet, if we examine our thinking, we will see that our worries and anxieties are mostly about things we can do nothing about.

Instead of worrying about things that are not under our control, if we spend our time acting only on what is within our control, our lives will change in a way we can't even imagine now.

Let's see what this means. Consider the following examples:

- *You have lost your job.* You worry about it, getting angry and frustrated. Yet this situation is not within your control, and you are simply making yourself unhappy. But many other things are within your control. You can enjoy a meal. You can enjoy the few days between jobs. You can apply for a new job. You can send the word out that you are now available for new work. Instead of worrying about the loss of your job, you can do many things that will improve your life.

- *You are diagnosed with a disease like cancer.* You may feel devastated and ask yourself, "Why me?" You may go over what you have done wrong in your mind. But you already have the disease and can do nothing about it. Yet, there are many things under your control. You can decide to enjoy your life as much as possible, no matter what happens. You can see a specialist. You can change any unhealthy habits. All these adjustments are within your control and will likely improve your life.

If you attempt to do something about both what is within your control and what is not, you may end up achieving nothing. Therefore, you clearly need to distinguish between the two. So what things are within your control and what are not?

- *Things that are within your control:* what you believe, what you desire or hate, what you are attracted to and what you try to avoid. You have complete control over these, so they are free and not subject to restraint or hindrance. They concern you because they are within your control.

- *Things that are not within your control:* your body, property, reputation, status, and the like. Because they are not within your total control, they are weak, slavish, subject to restraint, and in the power of others. They do not concern you because they are outside your control.

Our window of control may appear small, but it is large enough to lead us to freedom, happiness, and serenity.

Everything that happens around you or to you is part of reality, presented to you. How you deal with these things will determine whether you will be happy and free or miserable and bound. You need to deal with what happens to you using things that are within your control. You will be hindered and frustrated when you try to deal with them using things not within your control. If you lead your life confining yourself only to things within your control, no one can stop you from being free, happy, and serene.

ACTING EXCELLENTLY

To practice this principle effectively, you need four special skills, or four "excellences" (also known as virtues): *practical wisdom, moderation, courage*, and *justice*. We will come back to these later in this book.

Once you start confining your actions to what is within your control and practice practical wisdom, moderation, courage, and justice, you are on your way to a flourishing, happy life. Nothing can stand in your way.

TAKEAWAYS

Some things in life are within your control, and others are not. If you ignore what is not within your control and act on what is, your life will change for the better.

TRY THIS SIMPLE EXERCISE

Scan your mind and identify any concerns, worries, or anxieties you are currently facing. Write them down.

Look at each one. Is doing something about it within your control? If no, why worry about it? If yes, just do it and be done with it.

In either case, your concerns, worries, and anxieties serve no purpose.

The magic formula of Marcus Aurelius

How to get what you want right now

If someone told you that it is possible for you to have everything that you have been trying so hard to get, right now, you would probably head for the nearest exit. I certainly would. We all know the pitch of snake-oil salespeople. Their products never work.

But what if the person who told you this was the beloved Stoic emperor, Marcus Aurelius? Now, that's different. Marcus Aurelius is not given to making wild statements. So let's listen to him, even if we find it difficult to believe his claim:

> You have been trying to reach many things by taking the long way around. All these things can be yours right now if you stop denying them to yourself. All you have to do is let go of the past, trust the future to providence, and direct the present to reverence and justice.
>
> Marcus Aurelius, *Meditations* 12.1

Can it be that simple? Let's examine whether there is any truth to his claim. Where do our problems come from? They come mostly from our worries about the past and anxieties about the future—something that already has happened or something that might happen in the future. Neither of them exists right now.

What has already happened is not under your control now. Neither is what is going to happen in the future. Who could have predicted the effects of COVID-19? Or the Russo-Ukrainian War or the Israeli–Hamas conflict? When the past and the future are not under our control, what purpose is served by worry or anxiety?

As Marcus points out:

> You only live in the present, this fleeting moment. The rest of your life is already gone or not yet revealed.
>
> Marcus Aurelius, *Meditations* 3.10

Imagine a life in which you refuse to worry about anything that happened in the past and refuse to be anxious about anything that might happen in the future. If your past stops haunting you and the future stops scaring you, what do you have left? Just this moment. If you can live this moment well and the next moment and the next with out fear or anxiety, what else could you ask for? Wouldn't your life be well lived?

WHY WE SHOULD LIVE IN THE PRESENT

Our present worries have a short shelf life. But we prolong them and create our own misery. Seneca describes this very vividly:

> Wild animals run from the dangers they actually see, and once they have escaped them, worry no more.

> We, however, are tormented alike by what is past and
> what is to come. A number of our blessings do us
> harm, for memory brings back the agony of fear while
> foresight brings it on prematurely. No one confines his
> unhappiness to the present.
>
> Seneca, *Moral Letters* 13

Similarly, when we decide to be unhappy now because we are anxious about the future, our mind tells us that, because we may have problems in the future, we should start being unhappy right now.

> What I advise you to do is, not to be unhappy before
> the crisis comes; since it may be that the dangers [...]
> will never come upon you. They certainly have not yet
> come. Accordingly, some things torment us more than
> they should, and some torment us when they should not
> torment us at all. We are in the habit of exaggerating,
> or imagining, or anticipating sorrow.
>
> Seneca, *Moral Letters* 13

Let me give the last word to Epictetus:

> There is only one way to be happy. Keep this thought
> ready for use morning, noon, and night. Give up the
> desire for things not under your control.
>
> Epictetus, *Discourses* 4.4

There you have it. The only way to get what you want out of life is not to worry about the past or be anxious about the future but to handle what is right in front of you. And it can be done right now. It is the magic formula for getting what you want out of your life.

TAKEAWAYS

All our worries and anxieties are the result of something that has happened or something that might happen in the future. But we don't control our past or our future. So, no purpose is served by being worried or being anxious. If you let go of what is not under your control, your life will start flowing well.

TRY THIS SIMPLE EXERCISE

If you want to see how much of our life we waste, which involves living in the future and the past, try this simple exercise.

Close your eyes. Think of anything that is bothering you. See it clearly in your mind's eye. See how bad it makes you feel.

After a minute, open your eyes. Look around you. Observe what you see. Look out. Maybe the sun is shining. Or it may be raining. Maybe you hear some sounds, maybe not.

No matter what it is, it has nothing to do with the turmoil of your mind. Your worries and anxieties are happening entirely in your mind. It is because your mind is wandering away from the present, into the past or into the future.

The power to change your life

Your life can change when you realize what you think of as facts are opinions

A LESSON IN ATTITUDE ADJUSTMENT

Many years ago, I went shopping with a friend. It was Christmas time, and the mall was crowded. I didn't enjoy it at all. I can't say that I "hated" the crowd, but I did not like negotiating my way through it, was bothered by the loud music, and did not enjoy waiting for a long time to get to the cash register. I turned to my friend to complain, but she beat me to it. With an enthusiastic smile, she said, "I love shopping around this time. So many people here are having fun shopping to celebrate the festive season with their loved ones! I'm sure they have other problems and cares, but now they are happy, enjoying the break, and preparing to celebrate! And the Christmas songs that are being played! This is the best time to be here!"

The very things that annoyed me pleased her. Then I spotted a big bookstore. "Let's go in here for a while," I said. I can get lost in a bookstore and easily spend an entire afternoon there. We went into the bookstore, but after twenty minutes, she said, "Let's go. I want to see the Christmas decorations outside."

I was disappointed. I didn't realize then that my friend was teaching me a lesson in Stoicism without meaning to. I was learning a lesson, although it did not become clear to me until years later when I came across this:

> If you are pained by anything external, the pain is not due to the external thing. It is due to the way you look at it.
>
> Marcus Aurelius, *Meditations* 8.47

It was not the crowd and the loud music that were bothering me. I judged crowds and loud music as annoying, so they bothered me. It was not my having to leave the bookstore that disappointed me; it was my judgment that I should spend a long time there. I thought that the crowd was annoying and the bookstore was pleasant. No. They were my judgments, my opinions. It was my opinions that were making me unhappy. My friend had different opinions, so she was happy. I could have been as happy as her if I didn't have my judgments. What can I do about it? Simple, says Marcus Aurelius:

> Forget the belief "I've been harmed," and you won't feel harmed. Reject your sense of injury, and the injury itself disappears.
>
> Marcus Aurelius, *Meditations* 4.7

All you have to do is drop your judgments, and your misery will disappear. The best part is that it can be done in a moment.

WHERE DO OUR OPINIONS COME FROM?

How is it that we hear and see the same thing but have different opinions, which leads us to happiness or misery? Where do opinions come from? Opinions come from a wide variety of sources, such as:

- *Things we habitually do without paying attention.* We may find sleeping on one side of the bed more comforting than the other, or we may prefer sitting in our favorite chair that is no different from another similar chair. We develop an attachment to what we have been habitually doing. We are constantly subjected to religious, cultural, and social narratives. We internalize them and base our opinions on those stories.

- *Things we have experienced.* Our past experiences can color our opinions. If we have grown up in a hostile environment, it is easy to see most neutral events as potentially hostile.

- *Things that have a biological basis.* Biologically, we are programmed to sense threats in our environment. Many such threats may be false alarms. Some of us are more prone than others to interpret many things as threats.

The Stoics said that it doesn't matter where they come from; we have control over them and can change opinions at any time. Even when our reaction is instinctive—such as fear or anger when we perceive danger—we can pull back, pause, and reconsider.

THE POWER TO CHANGE YOUR LIFE

This deceptively simple Stoic lesson has the power to change your life. We go through life fully believing that things that happen, and the people we have to deal with, cause our problems. We never stop to think that the *same events and the same people who make us unhappy make others happy.* Once we realize that the same events and people that annoy us please others, and vice versa, we see we hold the key to making many things that bother us disappear instantly. We can change our lives not only in minor ways but in major ways as well.

We may see some logic in this, but we may still wonder how it can possibly change our lives. That's because we don't know how much of our lives is ruled by our judgments and opinions.

> Everything depends on opinion; ambition, luxury, and greed hinge on opinion. It is according to opinion that we suffer. A man is as bad as he has convinced himself that he is.
>
> Seneca, *Moral Letters* 78

Epictetus takes it further and shows how opinions govern most of our lives:

> What is misfortune? An opinion. What is subversion, dissension, complaint, blame, accusation, or foolish talk? These are all mere opinions, things that are not subject to our choice. If you transfer your opinions to what is within your choice, I guarantee you peace of mind, no matter what is happening around you.
>
> Epictetus, *Discourses* 3.3

We dredge up the past and become heroes in our tragic stories. So, what do we do about it? You may say, "None has ever been worse off than I. What suffering, what evil I have endured! No one thought I would recover. How often have my family neglected me, and the physicians seen me!"

Seneca asks: So what?

> Even if all this is true, it is over and gone. What benefit is there in reviewing past sufferings and in being unhappy just because once you were unhappy? Besides, everyone adds much to his own suffering and tells lies to himself.
> That which was bitter to bear is pleasant to have gone through; it is natural to rejoice at the ending of this pain.
>
> Seneca, *Moral Letters* 78

We should realize that the past is over and done with, no matter what has happened. What is holding us back is not the past but our opinion that it was painful. If we had a painful past, shouldn't we celebrate that it is over? Most of us believe that other people and events around us make us react the way we do. We don't realize it is how we react to what happens to us that causes all our problems:

> We are not disturbed by what happens to us but by our opinion of those things.
>
> Epictetus, *Encheirdion* 5

TAKEAWAYS

1. We believe that other people upset us or make us angry.
2. But it is not so. Two people can be in the same situation when something happens. One may be upset by it, and the other may not be.
3. What upset us is not what happened but what we thought of it.
4. Your life can change when you realize that most of what you think as reality is simply your opinion of it.

15

TRY THIS SIMPLE EXERCISE

Stoics believed that most of our problems, large or small, would disappear once we realize the real cause of our troubles—our opinions and judgments. This is because we are mostly unaware of the source of our problems.

Let's start with something small. For example:

A friend says something mildly critical of you. Your immediate response could be defensive. Hold back. See that your response has arisen because of your judgment that it was unfair. Haven't you been mildly critical of others without meaning to be unfair? Why not change your opinion and see it as something harmless?

A guest arrives late for your sit-down dinner. You are annoyed because you think she has been disrespectful to your other guests. Again, see this as your opinion. The guest may have arrived late because an accident held up traffic. Or because of some other thing that was not under her control.

Move on to more difficult things. For example:

Someone whose mannerisms bother you.

Someone you can't stand because of their political views.

Things that "ruin things" for you, such as rain when you are on vacation, a noisy couple in an upscale restaurant.

And even more difficult things. For example:

You don't get the promotion, but your "undeserving" colleague does.

You go for your annual checkup, and the results are not good.

As you move from the easy to the more difficult ones, pay attention to your opinion's role in creating your suffering. When your colleague gets a promotion, would you still suffer if you believe she deserved it? If your annual checkup is not good, would you still suffer if you didn't believe it *should be* good?

As we become more conscious of our opinion's role in creating our suffering, we can gradually free ourselves from the shackles of our opinions and become free of unnecessary suffering.

Actions that shape us

What we do willingly, what we do unwillingly,
and what we postpone doing

EVERYDAY ACTIONS

Sometimes, we act willingly, sometimes reluctantly, and sometimes, we try to avoid acting for as long as possible. What is the
difference between these three categories of action? What can
we do to ensure that we act and that, when we act, our actions
help us live better?

1. *Actions we do willingly*: These are actions that make
   us feel good—for example eating, drinking, watching
   TV, and going to a movie or a ballgame. We are eager
   to take these actions.

2. *Actions we do reluctantly*: These are actions that may
   have negative consequences if we don't do them—for
   example going to work, getting up in the morning, or
   doing our tax returns. We may not be that thrilled to
   take these actions, but we act anyway because unpleas-
   antness might follow if we don't.

3. *Actions we need to take but keep putting off*: These are
   actions that need taking but have no deadlines—they

range from cleaning the house to helping others, contributing to society, and being in harmony with everything. We tend to postpone taking these as long as possible, maybe even forever.

We spend most of our time doing the actions that make us feel good. Given the choice between (1) and (2) above, we will choose (1) most of the time. Where *actions that need doing* (3) are concerned, we are not eager to do them unless circumstances directly or indirectly force us.

Are we right to indulge in actions that make us feel good because they are immediately rewarding and to reluctantly go along with actions that have negative consequences if not taken? Or should we spend more time on our "low-priority" actions with no deadlines that need doing?

1. What we do willingly

Is it OK to do whatever feels good? Is there anything wrong with going to a movie or a ballgame or spending money on expensive things because doing so makes us feel good? Stoics looked at these things and asked a simple question: "Does this action make me virtuous, or does it prevent me from being virtuous?" They concluded that things like money, entertainment, eating and drinking, in and of themselves, are neither virtuous nor vicious. So, they called them "indifferents."

But "indifferents" *could* lead to non-virtuous results. For example, drinking a glass of wine feels good. But if we continue drinking, it leads to drunkenness, which is against the Stoic virtue of moderation. Money can lead to either virtuous action (like helping others with it), vicious action (like using money to hurt others), or indifferent action (like spending it on neutral things that make you happy).

> Things themselves are indifferent, but the use that we
> make of them is not indifferent.
>
> Epictetus, *Discourses* 2.2

So, when you are about to act on something that feels good, your focus should be on whether it will lead to undesirable (non-virtuous) consequences. When you feel like acting on something that makes you feel good, don't think whether the action itself is good or bad. Instead, think about how to be skilled so your actions don't lead to undesirable consequences.

> [Skillful ballplayers] don't consider the ball good or bad;
> they only consider how to throw and catch it. Grace,
> skill, speed, and expertise lie in that.
>
> Epictetus, *Discourses* 2.5

In short, nothing is wrong with doing what feels good provided (1) it is not vicious, and (2) it does not lead to undesirable or non-virtuous results.

2. What we do reluctantly

There are things that we don't choose to do. But we don't have a choice because we may face unpleasant consequences if we don't. We may not want to get up in the morning, but if we don't, we may be late. We don't like filling in our tax returns; if we don't, we may face penalties. So we postpone, do them reluctantly, and have a miserable time doing them. Most such tasks are "externals."

Stoics have an interesting perspective on such tasks. If a task has to be done, then your choice is not between doing it or not doing it. Your choice is between doing it feeling cheerful or doing it feeling miserable. Why do you want to choose misery over cheerfulness? Wouldn't it make more sense to do it cheerfully?

Imagine you are tied to a moving cart. Would it make more sense to start walking with the cart willingly or be dragged along?

> When a dog is tied to a cart, if the dog follows the cart willingly, its spontaneous act coincides with necessity, but if it does not want to follow the cart, it will be compelled in any case. So it is with human beings, too: even if they do not want to, they will be compelled in any case to follow what is destined.
>
> Cleanthes (also attributed to Zeno)

And again:

> Fate leads the willing and drags the unwilling.
>
> Seneca, *Moral Letters* 107

When you have no choice, would you choose to follow willingly or to be dragged along? Doing anything reluctantly lowers the quality of your output and damages the quality of your life. Here is a shortcut to improve the quality of the actions in your life and increase your sense of well-being: *Whenever you don't have a choice of not doing something, choose to do it willingly.*

3. What we need to do but put off doing

What we put off is a very important group of actions. Here, I am not talking about indifferents, which are a matter of choice, such as "I want to learn Finnish someday." I am talking about things like:

"I should clean the house. I will do it sometime."

"I want to do some voluntary work to help others, but not just yet."

"I have to be in touch with my friend, but I will call her sometime."

"I have to help people in need. I will do it when I earn more."

"I would like to lead a simple life, but I haven't got around to doing anything about it now."

Why is this category of action important? These *actions need doing*, and they tend to be virtuous. They include actions that Stoics would consider as duties. They could be as simple as making your bed in the morning or as complex as organizing a charity event. They touch upon actions that deal with being wise, just, and cosmopolitan. No one can force us to be wise, be just, or be cosmopolitan. No one can force us to do our duties. So, it is easy to put off actions like this indefinitely. But that would be a mistake. Actions belonging to this category contribute to our happiness and well-being. So heed to the advice of Marcus Aurelius:

What do I have to complain about if I'm going to do what I was born for—the things I was brought into the world to do?

Marcus Aurelius, *Meditations* 5.1

You don't even have to "like" doing what you know you need to do. You just have to do it.

Do what you must; let happen what may.

Epictetus, *Discourses* 1.1

There is no apparent reward for these actions or punishment for not doing them, so we postpone them. But they contribute to our well-being, lasting happiness, and a life well lived.

DEALING WITH THE THREE CATEGORIES OF ACTION

1. *What we do willingly:* These tend to be indifferents. *Feel free to do them as long as the action is not vicious or does not have non-virtuous consequences.*

2. *What we do reluctantly:* These tend to be externals. Whenever you don't have a choice of not doing something, choose to do it willingly.

3. *What we need to do but put off doing:* These tend to be virtuous actions and duties. Train yourself to do them whether you like doing them or not.

TAKEAWAYS

Our actions are of three types: things we do willingly, what we do reluctantly, and what we postpone doing.

1. What you do willingly, you can continue to do if they do not harm us anyway.

THE POWER TO CHANGE

2. When you do something reluctantly, ask yourself if you have a choice in the matter. If you have not but to do it, choose to do it willingly. There is no point in struggling against the inevitable.

3. If what you put off is a virtuous or beneficial action, train yourself to do it, whether you like it or not.

TRY THIS SIMPLE EXERCISE

Every morning, think of three things you have been postponing doing (they can be as simple as organizing your closet or calling a friend you haven't been in touch with for a long time). Write them down and do them.

Practice this for a few days—you will notice an increase in your sense of well-being.

Acts of power

Acts have power when you focus on what's within
your control and not the outcome

ACTIONS VS. OUTCOMES

Acts have power when we fully concentrate on the act, not
the outcome. This may contradict many things we have been
taught, such as "Be results-focused" and "Only winning matters." What is the difference between focusing on actions and
focusing on outcomes? Why is focusing on acts more important than focusing on outcomes?

I know of a talented young chef whose dream it was to create
his own restaurant to showcase his culinary skills. He didn't
have enough money, but that didn't stop him. For the next few
years, he saved every penny he could. It helped, but not enough
to open his dream restaurant. However, he had saved enough
money and had such a reputation as a rising star that he was
easily able to borrow a large sum of money to open his own
restaurant. This was in early 2020.

Within months, restrictive regulations came into effect because
of COVID-19. First, people were asked to wear masks, and then
they were not even allowed to go out unless it was for essential

business. Restaurants started closing down. Our young chef had to pay back his heavy loan to the bank and pay his lease to the landlord. He had sunk all his savings in the restaurant, but no money was coming in. The government helped him financially to a certain extent, and the landlord was patient—for a while. As the pandemic went on indefinitely, the young chef had no choice but to close his restaurant to stop the financial bleeding and declare bankruptcy. He became very bitter, and as far as I know, he never recovered from his misfortune. He had his whole life ahead of him, yet he chose to give up in bitterness.

Let's go back in time to 1914. A 67-year-old inventor in New Jersey saw 11 buildings in his plant, which he built over a quarter of a century, go up in smoke. Because the plant contained many chemicals, the fire could not be put out quickly. According to *The World*, the loss was $7 million, although the plant was insured only for about $2 million (later estimates put the loss around $23 million). You would think this was a devastating loss for a 67-year-old man, but when reporters interviewed him, he said, "I'm pretty well burned out, boys. But I'll start all over again tomorrow." And he did. Here are some of the things he invented *after* the fire destroyed 11 buildings in his plant: alkaline storage batteries, concrete houses, warfare technologies, and an improved phonograph. Even if you are unfamiliar with this incident, I'm sure you would have guessed the inventor's name. It is Thomas Edison.

ACTS OF POWER VS. THOUGHTS OF WEAKNESS

What is the difference between our young chef and Thomas Edison? Both were talented in their fields. Both faced sudden misfortune. One became bitter because he focused only on the outcome over which he had no control, while the other continued to be successful because he was totally focused on the action over which he had control. Our chef could not have predicted the onset of COVID-19, and Edison could not have predicted the fire. The chef was defeated because he was focused on the outcome, which was not under his control, but Edison emerged victorious because he focused on what was under his control—his next action. *Our acts have power when we act on what is under our control.*

> If you deal with only those things that are under your control, no one can force you to do anything you don't want to do; no one can stop you. You will have no enemy, and no harm will come to you.
>
> Epictetus, *Encheiridion* 1

But what happens when we focus on the outcome over which we have no control?

> If you think you can control things over which you have no control, then you will be hindered and disturbed. You will start complaining and become a fault-finding person.
>
> Epictetus, *Encheiridion* 1

The chef's actions were not acts of power. If he had chosen otherwise, he could have picked himself up and worked for someone else until he rebuilt his capital as he did the first time and could have bounced back. Instead, he was consumed by things he had lost, over which he had no control. His thoughts became acts of weakness. He was "hindered and disturbed, and he started complaining and becoming a fault-finding person"— just as Epictetus predicted.

TURNING THOUGHTS OF WEAKNESS INTO ACTS OF POWER

How do we turn our thoughts of weakness into acts of power? By shifting our focus from what we cannot control (e.g. the plant burning down) to what we can control. (e.g. rebuilding it).

> Not being able to govern events, I govern myself, and if they won't adapt to me, I'll adapt to them.
>
> Michel de Montaigne, "On Presumption," *Essays*

Acts of power are effective and also therapeutic because we substitute them for despair. Our power to choose is far more important than what happens to us.

> Externals are outside my power. My choices are within my power. Where will I find the good and the bad? Within me, in things that are my own.
>
> Epictetus, *Discourses* 2.5

> Where is the good? In our choices. Where is the bad? In our choices.
>
> Epictetus, *Discourses* 2.16

It is not COVID-19 or the fire that made things good or bad. It's the choice between focusing on the outcome not under our control (as the chef did) and focusing on what is in our control (as Edison did) that made things good or bad. In every misfortune, we have a choice: to focus on what we don't control or to act on what we do. We are challenged to choose between thoughts of weakness and acts of power.

Don't focus on what happened. Focus on what you can do about it.

Only your choice matters. Only your choice to focus on what you control at any moment can turn thoughts of weakness into acts of power.

TAKEAWAYS

1. We have control over our actions, not the outcomes.
2. No matter what the outcome is, if you keep focusing only on your actions, your acts will have power.
3. Choose acts of power over thoughts of weakness.

TRY THIS SIMPLE EXERCISE

Think of something that is bothering you and causing you to feel stuck. You feel stuck because it is not under your control, and you are focusing on what you cannot control. The situation could be anything: the prospect of losing your job, an impending divorce, an unfavorable medical diagnosis, being criticized by your boss, or anything else. You feel stuck because, most likely, you can't do anything about the outcome.

Now think of one thing—however small—that you can do that *is* within your control. For example, updating your résumé and looking for job opportunities (losing your job), making the divorce amicable and not acrimonious (an impending divorce), looking for the best option for a cure (an unfavorable medical diagnosis), or understanding why you were criticized and what you can do about it (being criticized by your boss) are all acts of power. They will take you from your thoughts of helplessness to a much better place—a place of strength.

A shortcut to a better life

Dropping your "if only" thoughts

A QUICK WAY TO IMPROVE THE QUALITY OF YOUR LIFE

Would you like to know a quick way to improve the quality of your life? Just drop all the "if only" thoughts that cross your mind.

Let me explain.

A well-to-do, but not wealthy, friend told me about a wonderful opportunity he missed a few years ago. It went something like this. He was invited to participate in a once-in-a-lifetime investment opportunity open only to a select few. He was invited to this meeting only because he knew the opportunity's sponsor. (This was before the time of online meetings; he had to go to a different city to participate in a face-to-face meeting.) He had the option of going a day earlier or arriving on the day of the meeting, and he decided to take the flight on the day of the meeting. If everything had gone right, he would have arrived an hour before the meeting. Unfortunately, the flight he was about to take developed a mechanical problem at the last minute, and it was cancelled. No other flight would get him to the meeting on time. So he went home and didn't think much of it.

A few months later, he learned that his missed investment opportunity was so exceptional that everyone who invested in it became multimillionaires. He concluded his narrative by saying that his life would have been so different *if only* he had taken the earlier flight.

"If only I had taken the earlier flight ..."

I don't meet him often, but when I do, he generally brings up this story and imagines (and wants me to imagine) how wonderful it would have been "if only" he had taken an earlier flight all those years ago. There is nothing unusual about my friend. We all act this way in our daily lives. No matter who we are, we all have similar thoughts. If we examined our thoughts, we would see many of them are of the type:

"If only I had accepted the other job ..."

"If only I had married the other person ...

"If only I had started investing earlier ..."

"If only my father hadn't been so harsh ..."

Such "if only" thoughts can take different guises. For example, here are some variations of "if only" thoughts:

"I should have accepted the other job offer."

"It is stupid of me not to have taken the other job."

"I regret not taking the other job."

"What was I thinking when I turned down the other job?"

This way of thinking is not uncommon. We talk to others this way. When we do, they immediately jump in and support our thoughts, especially if they are our friends. Some may disagree with us, but no one will likely say we are talking nonsense. Yet, such thoughts are nonsensical and impede a happy, fulfilled life. How so?

Although we may think that the "if only" thoughts are harmless, they hold us back in many ways. They interfere with our happiness and prevent us from moving forward with our lives. Here is how:

1. Planting our feet firmly in the past

For starters, "if only" thoughts firmly plant our feet in the past so we can't move forward easily. These thoughts assume that we could somehow change the past. It is obvious that it is too late for my friend to have taken an earlier flight. To say "If only I had taken an earlier flight" is nonsensical and meaningless. We cannot travel back to the past. Our missed flights will remain missed flights forever. There's no way to change that. The time you spend regretting the past comes from the time you could spend building your future.

> You look at the past and think about what you lost instead of looking ahead and seeing what you can achieve.
>
> Seneca, *Moral Letters* 194

You can avoid living in the past by realizing that you can live only in the present.

> Forget everything else. Keep hold of this alone and remember it: Each of us lives only now, this brief instant. The rest has been lived already or is impossible to see.
>
> Marcus Aurelius, *Meditations* 3.10

We can only live in the present, this brief moment. Yet our "if only" thinking pretends we could somehow change our past. This is illogical and absurd. We cannot move forward when mentally trying to move backward in time.

2. Trying to control the things that we cannot

One of the most unproductive things we can do is try to control what we cannot. We know this to be true but fail to apply this principle consistently.

> Do not waste your time on what you cannot control or influence.
>
> Marcus Aurelius, *Meditations* 8.49

Whatever happened in the past—whether it was missing a bus two minutes ago or being involved in an accident 20 years ago—cannot be changed now. It is not under our control. Trying to control what cannot be controlled can result only in regret, self-pity, anger, or bitterness. It cannot change the past. Why waste our time going over things we cannot control instead of spending it on things we can?

3. Trying to live backward

When you say "if only," it is based on your current knowledge. When my friend felt that "if only" he had taken the flight a day earlier, he would be financially independent now, he was applying his current knowledge to the past. If he had taken the earlier flight and had taken advantage of the opportunity, it is quite possible that it could have gone sour, making him lose his money. It could have worked against him. In this case, he would have probably said, "If only I had not gone there, I would be much better off now." Everyone would have invested in Apple if they had known that a modest investment some 30 years ago would have made them rich. But there was no way of knowing that for sure. That's the meaninglessness of the "if only" thinking—pretending that we could apply our current wisdom to things in the past.

> Life can only be understood backwards, but it must be
> lived forwards.
>
> Sören Kierkegaard, *Journals*

4. Thinking you had a choice when you had none

If you say, "If only I had done that," the question is "Why didn't you?" You did what you did because, given the circumstances, that's the best you could have done. If you could have done otherwise, you would have. When my friend decided to go on the day of the meeting, he did so because (1) he didn't want to waste his time taking an earlier flight; (2) he could not have known that his plane would be subject to mechanical problems; and (3) he could not have known the investment would be exceptional. Given all this, his only logical choice at that time was to take the flight he did. At any time, we can only act on the information we have, taking our temperament into account.

When we have an impulse to do something, it is because we feel it is to our advantage. It is impossible to consider something to our advantage and do something else. Or consider something right and have an urge to do something else.

Epictetus, *Discourses* 1.18

No matter what we do, we only try to do our best given our knowledge and mental state while acting. We had no choice. We could not have done anything else at that time. Our only choice is to behave differently in the future if we choose to do so.

TAKEAWAYS

1. Our "if only" thoughts try to fix the past. But the past is over, and we can't go back and fix it.

2. "If only" thoughts make us believe that we can apply what we know now to the past. We don't have this choice.

3. Even if we can redo the past, it doesn't guarantee better outcomes. When we change one thing in the past, many other things also change.

4. Dropping your "if only" thoughts is a shortcut to a better life.

TRY THIS SIMPLE EXERCISE

Clearly, "if only" thinking is irrational and interferes with our ability to live effectively. The first step in getting rid of "if only" thinking is to become aware of it. Scan your mind and identify your "if only" thinking. It comes in many guises. Here are some examples of the many disguises of "if only" thinking:

"I should have done that" or "I shouldn't have done that."

"Why did I do that?" or "Why didn't I do that?"

"It was stupid of me to have done that" or "It is stupid of me not to have done that."

"It would have been better if I had done that" or "It would have been better if I had not done that."

"What was I thinking when I did that?" or "What was I thinking when I didn't do that?"

When you identify a few of such "if only" thoughts, look at them closely and see how irrational those thoughts are and how they disturb the tranquility of your mind. Let go of those thoughts because they serve no purpose.

Seize the day!

Four Stoic strategies to get the most out of the day

No one gets up in the morning thinking, "I want to waste my time today. I don't want to get anything done." We waste our time without meaning to, helplessly. We postpone things. We pretend we have an unlimited time supply, but we don't. We are always planning to live when life is passing us by. Yet, the only way to live well is to seize the day and live effectively today.

> Today well lived makes every yesterday a dream of happiness,
> And every tomorrow a vision of hope
> *Kalidasa*

But how exactly do we live well today? We try hard, and yet we don't even seem to have the time to do what is important, let alone create a well-lived life. No matter how hard we try, we end up with a backlog, which seems to grow only bigger. It is not that we don't have enough to get what is important to us done; we just fritter it away. We have all the time in the world if we use it correctly. Instead, we crave more time. More time won't help us if we keep misusing whatever time we have.

> The good in life does not depend on life's length but
> upon the use we make of it.
>
> Seneca, *On the Shortness of Life* 49

Do you want to live well today but don't quite know how? No problem, the Stoics are standing by to help you. They offered four major suggestions: *Eliminate the unnecessary, focus only on what needs doing today, avoid busywork,* and *be flexible.* Here is how:

1. Eliminate the unnecessary

Why do we waste so much time? It's because our life is full of junk. The clutter obscures our vision. We wander into blind alleys, not going anywhere in particular. We are pulled and pushed by random events. Realize this truth. Eliminate all that is unnecessary and ask yourself what you want to do today. Think about it and write it down. Do the things you want to do *before* doing random things. "Front-end load" important things. Keep the less important things for later.

> See clearly for yourself what is necessary and what is
> superfluous.
>
> Seneca, *Moral Letters* 49

Having a consistent vision is key. We will know how to eliminate the unnecessary when we have a consistent vision. When we eliminate the unnecessary, we will have enough time to do what we need to do.

2. Avoid busywork

We feel that we are too busy and don't have time to do everything. In reality, our time is taken up by activities that serve no purpose. It shows that our minds are restless and not at ease. Filling our time with activities that serve no purpose is useless.

> A love of ceaseless activity is not diligence. It is just the restlessness of a driven mind
>
> Seneca, *Moral Letters* 3

An agitated mind is not the same as an active mind. We should differentiate useless activities from focused actions. Focused actions are consistent with our vision as opposed to "activities," which are done for the sake of keeping ourselves busy.

3. Focus on today

One of the reasons why we are not productive is that we are worried about the future. But if we concentrate on what must be done today, we don't have to worry about what tomorrow might bring.

> Devote yourself to what should be done today, and you will not have to depend so much on tomorrow.
>
> Seneca, *Moral Letters* 1

If we take care of today, tomorrow will take care of itself. So, the only day we must be concerned about is today and what needs to be done today.

4. Be flexible

Just because you have a plan doesn't mean you should be rigid. You should stand by your plan only if it is a sound one. Otherwise, you should be flexible enough to change it if circumstances change or if you are wrong to begin with.

> We must stick with a decision.
> That applies only to a sound decision,
> not to any decision.
>
> Epictetus, *Discourses* 2.15

At the same time, we should not change our minds because we are fickle.

> We should not be afraid to change either our purpose
> or our position—as long as we don't let that flexibility
> become fickleness.
>
> Seneca, *On Tranquility* 9

There you have it. Follow these four guidelines, and the day is yours!

TAKEAWAYS

Four ways to seize the day:

1. Eliminate the unnecessary. Stick to the essentials.
2. Avoid busywork. Confine yourself to what matters.
3. Focus on today. Don't worry about the past or the future.
4. Don't be too rigid. Be flexible.

TRY THIS SIMPLE EXERCISE

Take a sheet of paper and write down everything you think that you have to do. Don't censor your thoughts. If anything comes up during the day, add it to this list.

Look at the list. Identify things that have to be done today. *Make it as few as possible.* This is your "will-do" list for the day. Decide to do the tasks on this list before you pay attention to anything else.

Take a look at the list again. How many items on this list do you truly intend to do? If you have done them all, repeat the exercise today and every day after that. See how it gradually goes out of control. If this happens, decide to seize the day and do whatever you intended to do for the day.

PART 2
WHAT ARE WE UP AGAINST?

OBSTACLES WE FACE ALONG THE WAY

So far, we have talked about some of the powerful Stoic principles that can yield big results. They are not difficult to understand and practice. Yet, once we start practicing these principles, we may find that things don't always go as smoothly as we expected. Many things will keep us from practicing these principles.

The silent systems of our mind will distract us. Our constant internal dialogue will challenge us. Our grasshopper mind will find something else that is shiny. The junk we have stored in our mind's attic will obscure what we need to do. Our drive to accumulate fame, fortune and power will overtake our efforts to lead a flourishing life. And our backseat drivers—foolishness, excess, fear, and injustice—will direct us to the wrong destination. These are the things we are up against when we try to follow the road to a well-lived life.

In Part 2, we will explore these obstacles that stand in our way and see how we can effectively deal with them.

Our silent systems of the mind

How to outwit them

WHY CAN'T WE DO THE RIGHT THING AT THE RIGHT TIME?

We say something and immediately regret it. We refuse to do someone a favor and wonder why we refused. We are angry at someone and then realize it was uncalled for. We ignore a hungry person who asks for help and feel guilty about it. We wonder why we fail to do the right thing at the time.

Stoics teach us that we cannot control what happens outside of us, but we have total control over how we respond to it. To be free and happy, we must focus on our reactions to things. Epictetus assured us that our "faculties of judgment, motivation, desire, and aversions" are under our control. The following quote summarizes the idea that we have control over how we respond to life situations:

> Between stimulus and response, there is a space. In that space, we have the power to choose our response. In our response lies our growth and our freedom.
>
> Attributed to Austrian psychiatrist Viktor Frankl

It is nice to think there is a gap between someone insulting us in public and our response to it. We can use this gap to formulate a rational response. If we could do that, we would always do the right thing at the right time.

But our experience does not seem to bear this out. Someone insults us, and we are there with counter-insults or justifications before they even finish their sentence. Someone lunges toward us on the street, and we show signs of fear. Even people who are usually calm can suddenly flare up when confronted with certain situations.

Why can't we seem to do the right thing at the right time?

The Stoic principle of control seems to contradict our experience. The silent systems of our mind seem to hijack its rational part and take control.

And all that makes us wonder. Where is the gap between the stimulus and the response? Can we really control our "faculties of judgment, motivation, desire, and aversions"? These are important questions because they go to the very heart of Stoicism: the question of what is under our control and what is not.

SILENT SYSTEMS OF THE MIND

Sprinkled throughout Stoic literature is also the idea that, although how we react to any situation is under our control, this does not apply to our initial reactions. Stoics acknowledge that our immediate negative responses are not always under our control. The response to any situation may be "up to us," but not necessarily our initial reaction to it.

> The first shocks of passion can be pardoned because they
> are involuntary.
>
> Seneca, *On Anger* 2.3.4

> When the feelings are transmitted to the mind, there
> is no point in trying to resist the sensation, which is
> involuntary.
>
> Marcus Aurelius, *Meditations* 5.26

> Emotions such as anger arise involuntarily and are a part
> of human nature.
>
> Epictetus, *Encheiridion* 5

So, while our rational response is up to us, we need to understand that silent systems of the mind can decide on our initial reactions. Scientists also confirm that we have hard-wired systems that are quick to react even before we become aware of them. Our "fight, flight, or freeze" reactions are automatic and take us over, short-circuiting our conscious response.

Stoics point out that we feel trapped because we accept silent systems of the mind (or "impressions") without examining them. Epictetus argued that "managing your impressions" is the single most important thing you can do.

But how do they become entrenched? Why do we react this way even after all these years? Why do we act as though we have no choice? We act the way we do because our automatic responses have positive reinforcements built into them. The first flush of anger feels good because of the adrenaline rush, and we go along with it without thinking. The flight response gets us to safety fast, and it doesn't occur to us that there may have been no danger in the first place. So, we get controlled more and more by the silent systems of our minds.

We may feel there is no way out, but the Stoics say there is. It takes practice, but it can be done.

Here is a three-pronged strategy to outwit the silent systems of our minds.

1. Create a gap

There may be no gap between something happening and our visceral response to it. However, we *can build a gap* by examining what is happening before reacting to our impressions, even if we cannot control our bodily responses. So, whenever you face a situation that makes you angry, fearful, upset, or defensive, don't respond immediately, even as you feel the emotion.

> Start by challenging everything that appears disagreeable. "You are only an appearance. Let me fully understand what you are."
>
> Epictetus, *Encheiridion* 1

If you don't want to "talk to your impressions," as Epictetus suggests, slowly take five deep and conscious breaths. Or, slowly count backward from ten to one. Intense emotions call for an immediate, unthinking response. The moment you divert your attention elsewhere, the intensity of emotion fades. The urgency to react diminishes. Now, you have created a gap between the stimulus and the response. This gives you an opportunity to react rationally to the situation.

2. Realize it is your responsibility

Once you succeed in creating the gap, realize that the negative emotion is your choice and is not likely to serve you well. Choose the most rational response.

> If you are pained by any external thing, it is not this
> thing that disturbs you but your own judgment about it.
> And it is in your power to wipe out this judgment now.
>
> Marcus Aurelius, *Meditations* 8.4

Don't keep telling yourself that it is all the other person's fault; he started it first, and you will show him, and so on. Instead, consider the benefits of not acting like a robot to the provocation. The solution is obvious once you realize that you suffer because of your reactions to what happened. You react differently in a way that benefits you. No one can make you angry or upset without your permission. Choose not to react negatively. Your mental health improves; maybe you didn't make the other person your enemy.

3. Mentally rehearse your reactions

Creating a gap between the stimulus and the response, between provocation and reaction, may be difficult when you are in the grip of emotion. You may say or do something even before you realize it. To make quicker progress, you may want to visualize yourself in such situations and rehearse how you will pull back, think, and choose your reaction. By rehearsing your responses, you will likely become aware of your emotions before you act on them, leading to regret. You want your reactions to be measured and rational. By practicing the mental habit of restraint, you will be able to be in control of yourself when you are provoked.

> Every habit and faculty is preserved and increased by corresponding actions: the habit of walking by walking, the habit of running by running. If you want to be a good reader, read; if you are a writer, write.
>
> Epictetus, *Discourses* 2.19

Yes, it will take time to be free of things we have been doing all our lives.

> No great thing is created suddenly any more than a bunch of grapes or a fig. If you tell me that you desire a fig, I answer you that there must be time. Let it first blossom, then bear fruit, then ripen.
>
> *Epictetus, Discourses* 1.15

TAKEAWAYS

1. We fail to say or do the right thing at the right time because the silent systems of our mind intervene and distract us from doing the right thing at the right time.

2. The three skills:

   a. creating a gap between the stimulus and the response

   b. rationally choosing how you would like to respond

   c. practicing in imaginary situations

   will go a long way in helping you manage impressions and counter the silent systems of the mind.

49

TRY THIS SIMPLE EXERCISE

Recall a time when you were angry, upset, worried, or anxious. Was this in reaction to some situation? If so, what is it?

Look at the situation again.

- What are other ways you could have viewed the situation?
- Are any of the other ways of looking at it better than how you saw it then?
- Could you have reacted differently?
- Do you see that you had a choice in that situation?

If you think you didn't have a choice, do you truly believe that no one could have handled the situation better?

Our constant internal dialogue

How to slow it down

OUR INTERNAL DIALOGUE

When we are not talking to someone, what do we do? We talk to ourselves. Even as you read this, you might be saying something to yourself like:

Yes, that's true.

No, I never talk to myself.

Very interesting. I never thought of that.

I wonder if this is true.

What has Stoicism to do with it?

Never heard anything so stupid.

I don't think Chuck knows what he is talking about.

So what?

Or something else. Who are you talking to? Yourself. Who is listening? You. What do you talk about? Anything that pops into your head.

Our mind is always chattering, judging, and analyzing. We never stop talking to ourselves from the time we get up until the time we go to sleep. And, of course, we talk to ourselves in our sleep, too.

THE TWO WORLDS WE LIVE IN

We live in two worlds: the one we think we live in and the one we actually live in. Our internal dialogue creates this alternative world. This is where we spend most of our time.

Try this: Think of some recent negative experience. Maybe you were angry or upset with someone. Maybe you were worried or anxious about something. Maybe you did something that you were deeply embarrassed about. Close your eyes and relive this experience. Continue doing so for the next couple of minutes. Now, open your eyes. Note what you see. Walls, windows, sunshine, rain, some noises? It can be anything, but it simply has nothing to do with what is going on in your mind.

Anyone in the room with you can probably see what you see, but the mental turmoil you experienced is your own. It doesn't exist "out there." While you live in a world of mental turbulence, someone next to you can live in a world of mental joy.

So, there are two worlds: one created by us and the other not created by us. Most of our problems are caused by living in the world of our creation and believing it is the only world.

SUSTAINING OUR INNER WORLD

Our inner world is unique to us. We create this world and sustain it by constantly and silently talking to ourselves.

The internal dialogue is what grounds people in the
daily world. The world is such and such or so and so
only because we talk to ourselves about its being such
and such and so and so.

Carlos Castaneda, *The Wheel of Time*

We add commentaries to everything we experience. It is not
"Someone bumped into me." It is "Some *careless idiot* bumped
into me." It is not "So-and-so did not talk to me." It is "So-and-so
doesn't like me and ignores me." It is not "My boss did not think
what I proposed was a good idea." It is "My boss *always denigrates*
my ideas." So we start living in a world in which people don't like
us, careless idiots bump into us, and bosses always denigrate us.
Such internal dialogues create and sustain an alternative world of
our own creation.

People are disturbed not by the things which happen but
by their opinion of them.

Epictetus, *Encheiridion* 5

The opinion that disturbs us is created by our thoughts and
nurtured by our internal dialogue.

THE ORIGIN OF INNER DIALOGUE: IMPRESSIONS

Objects that are far away look smaller. A stick, when partially immersed in water, looks bent. A loud voice in a small,
enclosed room sounds much louder than in a wide-open
space. The same food tastes much tastier when we are hungry
than when we are full.

"Things as they to us" are called impressions or appearances (*phantasiai*) in Stoicism. When your boss did not think what you proposed was a good idea, your impression was "I don't think my boss values me." We substitute our impression for reality and act as though our impression is the way the world is. It is like believing that the stick half-immersed in water is bent. Our impressions are unique to us. Other people may have different impressions of the same event. Our thoughts or "impressions" sustain the internal dialogue, creating an imaginary world in which we live.

SLOWING DOWN THE INTERNAL DIALOGUE

The alternative world we create using internal dialogue is usually a lot scarier than reality. Through our internal dialogue, we create and maintain our worries, anxieties, anger, fear, and depression. When we stop our internal dialogue, the world as we have come to know it collapses and disappears because it is a creation of our minds and doesn't really exist out there.

So, how do we slow down the internal dialogue?

It is not easy. Modern neurologists tell us that our minds are designed to produce thoughts continually, whether they are true or not. But we can always make a start and get far in stopping the internal dialogue. Even when we cannot, we can minimize its effect on our thinking.

1. Create a gap

We can easily mistake a piece of rope for a snake while walking on a poorly lit country road. But if we take a second look before accepting that impression, we might realize that it is only a rope. We can do the same when dealing with any impression: create a gap between the impression and our impression of the stimulus. We don't accept our first impression of anything. Instead:

> Start by challenging everything that appears disagreeable. "You are only an appearance. Let me fully understand what you are."
>
> Epictetus, *Encheiridion* 1

So, the first step in not getting carried away with your internal dialogue is to create a gap between your impression and its acceptance by you. If your impression is that your boss doesn't value you, this step creates a gap between your impression and the internal dialogue that expands on it.

2. Separate facts from commentary

Your impression of the person who didn't talk to you is that *she doesn't like you and ignores you.* What is fact, and what is commentary here?

Fact: the person did not talk to you.

Your commentary: she doesn't like you and ignores you.

You can apply this to all your impressions:

> His son has died. *What has happened? His son has died. Nothing more than that? Nothing more.*
>
> His ship has gone down. *What has happened? His ship has gone down.*

55

He has been taken off to prison. *What has happened? He has been taken off to prison.*

But the observation, "Things have gone badly for him" is something that each person adds for himself.

Epictetus, *Discourses* 3.8

3. Reassess the impression

You can now calmly reassess the situation. There are many ways to reassess your impression:

- You have lost your job, and you think it's bad. But this is not under your control. Since it is not under your control, you have nothing to do with it. There is nothing good or bad about it. That's the way it is.

- Someone doesn't talk to you, and you think she doesn't like you. There might be other reasons why she didn't talk to you. For example, she might have been distracted by something you are not aware of.

When we reassess our impressions, we will begin to see that we can't be sure that our impressions and the internal dialogue that follows have any validity.

Even when we are not certain whether a disagreeable impression is true or not, it is to our advantage to treat it as false. This will avoid unnecessary internal dialogue that can lead only to a more disagreeable state of mind.

TAKEAWAYS

1. Our minds are constantly chattering, whether we realize it or not. This is our internal dialogue.

2. Our internal dialogues distort the real world we live in. We should silence or slow down our internal dialogue to minimize the distortion.

3. We can minimize our internal dialogue by:

   a. creating a space between the stimulus and our actions

   b. separating facts from commentary

   c. reassessing our impression.

TRY THIS SIMPLE EXERCISE

Set your timer for three minutes. Take any topic of your choice. For the next three minutes, decide not to think about any subject other than this.

Note how many times your mind wanders away from the subject. This is your mind indulging in internal dialogue.

Repeat this exercise randomly until you realize that your mind is constantly chattering. If you keep doing this, the mental chatter will start to slow down.

Our grasshopper mind

How to rein it in

IN TEN SECONDS FLAT

You are walking down the street on a cold winter's day. You feel like going somewhere warm and pleasant on holiday. But you cannot think of it right now. That's because you loaned a large sum of money to your best friend when he lost his job a few months ago. Last month, he got another job, but you can't ask him to pay back the loan yet because his mother has become seriously ill, and he is struggling to pay her medical bills. Why should medicine be so expensive? It is all because pharma companies charge so much for essential medicines. Perhaps the government should regulate how much pharma can charge for essential drugs.

In ten seconds flat, you have gone from a cold winter's day to how much pharmaceutical companies charge for essential drugs and government regulations. Your mind hopped from a winter's day to a holiday to money problems, a friend losing his job, his mother, her illness, medical bills, pharmaceutical prices, and potential government regulations.

OUR GRASSHOPPER MIND

This is how our minds work. They jump from topic to topic. We all have a grasshopper mind.

Is it a problem? Not always. It is like driving a car on autopilot. It is OK if the highway is clear and the car doesn't exceed the speed limit. But what if the car suddenly starts hurtling at 120 miles an hour on a crowded highway, moving erratically? Now, it has become dangerous.

Our minds on autopilot do this quite often. One angry thought leads to another angry thought, and another and another before we are seething with rage. One negative thought leads to another negative thought, and another and another before we fall into depression. One anxiety-provoking thought triggers another anxiety-provoking thought and another and another before we see a bleak future ahead of us.

A grasshopper mind makes focusing on what is in front of us difficult. We dream of holidays when at work and think of work when on holidays. We are on the phone when at dinner. We text when we walk.

We know:

A rolling stone gathers no moss.

Publilius Syrus (attributed)

The grasshopper mind quickly takes us away from the present, where life is happening. Wouldn't it be better for us to be where our life *is* happening? Wouldn't it be a good idea to rein in our grasshopper minds so we can experience life more fully?

Let's see what suggestions Stoics offer to rein in our grasshopper minds.

1. Train yourself to choose

Remember when you were deeply involved in writing an important report, enjoying an exquisite meal, or playing a game? You were absorbed in whatever you were doing and unaware of anything else. Psychologists call this state the flow state. You can observe this kind of focus when professional athletes are playing, professional artists are doing their work, or even when children are absorbed in play. They are not *trying* to concentrate but concentrate. Such concentration is not the result of trying to control the grasshopper mind but immersing themselves in whatever they are doing.

> If you don't pause to consider what is involved, you will end up like a child: wrestler one minute, gladiator the next, actor one minute, musician the next. You will be like a monkey that imitates whatever comes its way, drawn by different things. You have not paid attention, and you have not thought things through. You are being casual and arbitrary.
>
> Epictetus, *Encheiridion* 29

The first step in training your mind is to decrease mind wandering. Initially, what you choose will not matter. However, once you become more practiced in choosing, you may want to choose things that align with your life's objectives. If you choose to chat with your friends on social media over having a dinner conversation with your family, do it so you can practice reining in your mind that hops from where you are to where you want to be. Train yourself to do whatever you do fully.

2. Once you have decided, stay with it

Once you have decided to do something—whether to eat dinner or help go to the gym—banish all other thoughts from your mind. Don't let your grasshopper mind second-guess your decision and go back and forth between what you have decided to do and what you have chosen not to do.

> You must always consider [...] how to spend no time over all other incoming impressions. This will happen [...] if you are free from all stray thoughts and from any deviation.
>
> Marcus Aurelius, *Meditations* 2.5

One of the reasons our mind goes from one thing to another is we keep second-guessing ourselves. A player cannot score a goal if, having decided to kick the ball in one direction, he starts wondering about the decision.

If your mind starts wandering, remind yourself that you had the choice but chose this one. When you go to a restaurant, you enjoy the dish you ordered without thinking about the dishes you didn't. So also, once you have chosen to do something, stop wasting time thinking about things you didn't choose to do.

Our minds' tendency to be everywhere—not just where we have chosen to be—will not get us anywhere.

> To be everywhere is to be nowhere.
>
> Seneca, *Moral Letters* 2

3. Choose what is worthy

I said that, initially, it wouldn't matter what you choose to pay attention to as long as you do it fully. But this is only to train your mind. What you choose to do does matter.

> "Where do I find good and evil?"
> "In your choices."
>
> Epictetus, *Discourses* 2.5

So, the first step in controlling a grasshopper mind is to rein it in. The next step is to ensure you choose the right things to focus on.

How do you know what is the right thing to focus on? You can think through what is important or ask yourself when the situation arises. If, during a meal, you are tempted to call someone, you can ask yourself, "What is more important? Do I want to enjoy my meal fully and savor the flavor and taste, or is it so critical my call cannot wait until I finish my meal?" If your family is important to you, you will not be tempted to text your friends when you are dining with your family. If being with nature is important to you, you will not be tempted to be on the phone while hiking.

Your choices follow from what is important to you. If you are obsessed with money, you will have no problem choosing between relaxing on vacation and calling your broker—you'll call your broker. If you are obsessed with your work, you will have no problem between being a workaholic and having a balanced work and life approach—you will choose to work. So, what you choose will depend on your values.

If you think a Stoic way of life is important, you would choose actions consistent with that vision. When you choose actions that are consistent with your vision, it is easier to stay focused. Grasshopper minds work overtime when we are not sure what is important to us in our lives.

TAKEAWAYS

1. Our minds naturally hop from one topic to another. This can create problems for us.
2. We can train our minds to rein in this tendency. Professional athletes and artists do it routinely.
3. The first step is to choose one thing and stay with it.
4. Once you succeed, choose things that are consistent with your values. When your mind wanders, remind yourself of the importance of remaining with what you have chosen.

TRY THIS SIMPLE EXERCISE

Start with any topic. Try to focus on the topic for a few minutes. Watch how your mind jumps from one topic to another.

Stop.

Watch what you are thinking about now.

Decide to think about that topic only and NOTHING ELSE for two minutes. Set your timer.

Were you able to focus on the topic for two minutes, or did your mind keep wandering? Repeat this exercise from time to time so you become aware of your mind wandering before it has gone too far.

Our junk in the mind's attic

How to clear it

We color our minds by what we repeatedly think. Angry thoughts produce more angry thoughts, anxious thoughts produce more anxious ones, and hopeful thoughts produce more hopeful ones.

The quality of our life is based on the quality of our thoughts.

> Your mind will resemble your frequently repeated thoughts because it takes on the hue of its thoughts.
>
> Marcus Aurelius, *Meditations* 5.16

Our recurring thoughts originate from what we store in the attics of our minds. They are mostly our unexamined impressions from the past. Let's take a closer look.

WHAT WE STORE IN OUR ATTICS

What do we store in our attics, basements, or storage facilities? Usually, it is things we don't know what to do with just yet. We don't examine them. We put them out of our minds by putting them out of sight. We think we have solved the problem. But these things remain there forever, only to create problems later.

Why do we do this? Why can't we get rid of the things that are not useful, fix the things that need fixing, and decide what to do with things we thoughtlessly store? We do these things mostly because we don't want to spend time deciding. Our indecision creates clutter and costs us resources.

Even more destructive is what we store in our mind's attic. *Here we store our unexamined impressions*, such as our prejudices, resentments, grievances, unrelated facts, and rumors. Collectively, they can be called "junk thoughts." We treat the junk in our mind's basement as something precious, even as it crowds out the thoughts that will help us lead a flourishing life. When we go about our lives, junk thoughts from the attics of our minds pop up to disturb our tranquility. What are these thoughts like?

I never get the breaks I deserve.

My neighbor is such a jerk.

If only my family was less dysfunctional.

I'm sure I won't have enough when I retire.

My boss is not very smart.

People are unfair.

We are often unaware that our mind's attic harbors such thoughts and color our reactions to events. So, we continue to blame external events for the state of our lives.

How do we deal with the attic of our mind?

CLEARING THE JUNK IN OUR MIND'S ATTIC

When I bought a house many years ago, a friend said, "Make sure you finish your basement. An unfinished basement is a junk magnet." That worked well for me. Let's see whether we can apply this wisdom to our mind's attic.

The junk we store in our mind's attic, such as grievances of things past, unexamined impressions, and imagined troubles of future happenings, is the source of our disturbance and fear. Seneca suggests that the key to tranquility and freedom is eliminating things that disturb and frighten us:

> Once we have driven away all things that disturb or frighten us, there follows unbroken tranquility and unending freedom.
>
> Seneca, *On the Happy Life* 3

Identifying all the junk stored in your mind's attic may be difficult because much of it could be hiding in the darkness, only to pop up and color your impressions. So, let's start now and be on guard.

1. See how the quality of your thoughts affects your judgments

Unexamined impressions are the main cause of unhappiness. We often act on unexamined impressions (such as "My boss doesn't like me," "I will be really happy when I make a million dollars," or "So-and-so is talking behind my back"). The quality of our thoughts is influenced by the thoughts we frequently repeat, which we store in and retrieve from our mental attic.

Because thoughts are colored by what we store in our mind's attic, let's look at our thoughts closely and fully.

Suppose you think: "My partner is unfair to me." Don't accept it right away. Look at it. What is the source of this impression? What caused it? How long have you had this impression? How long do you think you will continue to hold this impression? See how this impression is affecting how you see your partner.

> Always look at the whole thing. What is making an
> impression on you? Unpack it. Analyze its cause,
> its matter, its purpose, and its duration.
>
> Marcus Aurelius, *Meditations* 512.18

See how it colors your thoughts, affects your judgment, and causes you to act on distorted impressions. Become aware of the connection between the junk we store in our mind's attic, our distorted judgments, and the quality of our lives.

2. Be selective about thoughts that enter your mind's attic

We should be careful about what we store in our attic and guard it so that no unexamined impressions, biases, grievances, or prejudices can enter. This means we need to examine every thought and impression. Marcus Aurelius suggests you should not accept any thought or impression as true without examining it. If you decide a thought is false or inconclusive, refuse to store it in your mind's attic:

> You should be on guard against them at every moment.
> Whenever you detect them, you should eliminate
> them. Tell yourself, "This thought is unnecessary," or

"This one is destructive to the people around me,"
"These are not my true thoughts [they are just unexamined impressions]," or "This thought has got the better
of my divine part."

Marcus Aurelius, *Meditations* 11.19

For example, instead of accepting a thought like "What happened to me was unfair" or "My friend is thoughtless" and
putting it in your attic, ask yourself:

Does this thought deserve a space in the attic of my mind?

Doesn't it damage my relationships with others?

Do I really believe it?

Can't I rise above this?

Don't give any more rent-free space in your mental attic for
unexamined impressions of past grievances and future anxieties.
Ensure that nothing enters your mental attic until you examine
and approve it.

3. Use reason to filter out unexamined impressions

While it is difficult to identify all the grievances, prejudices,
resentments, and anxieties we have stored in the dark corners of
our attics, they routinely manifest in our daily lives. Whenever
we get angry or upset, become worried or anxious, or become
judgmental, the chances are some junk thought from our
mind's attic has taken over. So, we should immediately use reason to identify the junk stored in our attic. In short, we apply
reason to assess our impressions.

> [Reason] tries to delete the bad judgments entrenched
> in our minds as the result of misperceptions and to free
> us from them. It tries to introduce sound judgments in
> accordance with nature or to correct unsound judgments.
>
> Musonius Rufus, *Letter to Pankratides*

We should throw out the junk in the attic and replace it with sound judgments:

> We must try to free ourselves from these evils to the
> extent we are created to live in an orderly and decent way.
>
> Musonius Rufus, *Letter to Pankratides*

This is not a one-time effort. We have been accumulating mental junk all our life and nourishing it. Completely getting rid of it cannot be done overnight. It is a long process but a rewarding one.

TAKEAWAYS

We store unexamined impressions in our mind's attic. These are junk and stay indefinitely in our mind's attic and cloud our judgements. To clear the junk:

1. See how your judgments are affected by the quality of your thoughts.

2. Be selective about the thoughts that you let enter your mind's attic.

3. Use reason to filter out unexamined impressions.

TRY THIS SIMPLE EXERCISE

Think of an instance (preferably a recent one that you can clearly recall) where you were quick to get angry, upset, or judgmental. Review exactly what happened. What made this happen? Looking back, was it really as bad as you thought it was? See its connection to other times you felt the same way.

Do you see a pattern? Could you have handled it better? Was it—getting angry, upset, or judgmental—worth it? Look at the role the junk you stored in your attic (past conditioning, resentment, entitlement, etc.) played in creating the situation.

Decide to be careful what you let enter the attic of your mind.

Our quest for more

How do we stop exchanging our lives for excessive stuff?

I had breakfast with a friend at a central London hotel a few years ago. I have known him for a long time since he was a student at the London Business School. We had a pleasant conversation. Looking distinguished in his expensive bespoke suit, he talked about the millions he had made, his fancy house, his exotic travels, and his beautiful family. He wasn't bragging; he was just making conversation:

"Yours is a charmed life!" I said.

He smiled, paused for a moment, and replied, "Yes, Chuck, I have everything life has to offer—except life."

I wasn't expecting this. My friend is not given to introspection. So this, coming from him, surprised me. It got me thinking. I remembered the line from an old song.

> Life is what happens to you
> While you're busy making other plans.
> *Attributed to John Lennon*

It also reminded me of Seneca's view on our useless pursuits:

They finally realize how miserable the results of all they
have rushed through are and how they have left no
leisure for themselves. Then, they reflect on how futile
the things they pursued so busily were. When it is too
late, they feel what it is they have lost and why; old age
accuses them of being fools, making them realize the fact
through the testimony of their own lives.

Seneca, *On the Shortness of Life* 3

We acquire things like money, jobs, homes, family, and goods
to make our lives comfortable. So far, so good. But at some
point, acquiring stuff becomes the goal in and of itself. We
exchange our time for more stuff. But our lives are made of
time. So when we spend time getting more and more stuff, we
swap our lives for stuff, most of which doesn't enrich our lives.
My friend meant this when he said he had everything life has
to offer, except life. He was giving up his life to get more and
more things.

Why do we continue to do this? Why do we exchange something precious and limited, like our life, for stuff we can do
without? Why do we make money that we cannot spend in our
lifetime? Why do we spend more money on clothes when we
already have a closet full of them? Why do we work harder to
leave a legacy for our children than live the life we are given?

Stoics have the answers.

THE NATURE OF OUR DESIRES

Seneca, borrowing from Epicurus, said that we have two kinds
of desires:

- natural desires
- opinion-based desires.

Natural desires aim to fulfill our basic needs, which are things we need to exist, such as food, water, and shelter. *Opinion-based desires* arise only because we think they are desirable. For example, the desire for food when we are hungry is a natural desire. However, the desire for fancy, exotic, and expensive food is opinion-based. When thirsty, the desire for clean water is natural, but the desire for expensive imported bottled mineral water is opinion-based.

Natural desires

Objects of natural desires are easy to get and are inexpensive. Even if you are not well-off, you should be able to get something to eat, even if it is as basic as bread and water. Not only are they easy to get, but they also have natural limits. No matter how hungry you are, you can only eat so much food. No matter how thirsty you are, you can only drink so much water. You can wear only so many clothes at once and sleep in a single room to be safe from the elements. So, generally speaking, natural desires pose no threat to most of us.

Opinion-based desires

Opinion-based desires can be hard to get and expensive. They may be difficult to get and have no natural limits. You may buy a ready-to-wear suit for $300, a designer suit for $3,000, or a bespoke suit made from an exquisite material for $10,000 or more. Let's say that you can easily afford a $10,000 suit.

Nothing stops you from looking into getting an even more expensive suit made from a still higher-quality material—maybe at $30,000, outfitted by a renowned designer. The same is true for food—you can buy healthy, market-fresh vegetables and cook them for $10. Or go to an expensive restaurant run by a well-known chef and pay ten times as much. And, of course, there are more expensive restaurants when you look for them. This is also true of your house, car, furnishings, and so on.

> Natural desires are limited, but those which spring from
> false opinions can have no stopping point. The false has
> no limits. When you travel on the road, there must be
> an end, but if lost, your wandering is limitless.
>
> Seneca, *Moral Letters* 16

So, if we are not mindful, our opinion-based desires will take us over and run our lives for us. Then, we will have "everything in life, except life." Money and stuff cannot buy life, no matter how hard we try

HOW TO CULTIVATE YOUR LIFE, NOT YOUR STUFF

How do we cultivate our life instead of stuff? By keeping our opinion-based desires in check. Musonius Rufus, who taught Epictetus Stoicism, has some simple suggestions (Musonius Rufus, *Lectures*, 18–20). He asks, "Aren't all these things excessive and unnecessary? Can't we live and be healthy without all this?" Here are his specific suggestions:

- Choose inexpensive food over expensive food and easily available food over food that is difficult to get. Choose food suitable for humans over food that is not. Grains and other plants can nourish humans. Choose foods that need no cooking: seasonal fruits, some vegetables, milk, cheese, and honey. They are very easy to get.

- Protect your body modestly, not extravagantly. Wear clothing and shoes as you would armor: to protect the body, not to show off. The covering of the body should make it better and stronger, not weaker and worse.

- Because we build houses to protect ourselves from the elements, we should build them accordingly. The house should be moderate—just big enough for our needs.

- Keep your furnishings simple and functional.

When we thus reduce our opinion-based desires to a minimum, we will live a life on our terms and not fritter it away in the worship of money and stuff.

> A simple cot is no worse to lie on than a silver or ivory bed; a rough cloak is as good a bed cover as a purple or crimson spread. We can eat comfortably from a wooden table as we can from a silver one. We can drink from a ceramic cup and quench our thirst as well as we can from a golden cup.

Musonius Rufus in Stobaeus 4.28.20. Chapter 28: Household Management

This is not a call for austerity. It is a call to wake up and realize that the simple things of life are as good as, if not better than, things we desperately try to acquire while life passes us by.

TAKEAWAYS

1. Our life is made of time. When we use our time to acquire more and more stuff, we are swapping our lives for stuff and missing out on life.

2. Some desires, such as the desire for food, water, or shelter, are essential for survival. These desires have limits and are easy to satisfy.

3. However, desires that are not essential for survival, such as excessive wealth, power, and prestige, have no stopping point. They consume our lives.

4. To lead a vibrant life, we need to keep our runaway desires in check.

TRY THIS SIMPLE EXERCISE

List all the things that you want to acquire—maybe a new car, a bigger home, a better job, or something else.

Consider each one. Is this essential for your survival? If not, are you keeping these desires in check so they don't consume you and get in the way of you enjoying your life? Do you really need it?

Also, consider the price of the things you want to acquire—not just the money but the time you put in to get them. Do these things deserve the time you invest in them?

Temper your desires if you find them getting in the way of a vibrant life.

Our four backseat drivers:
1. Foolishness

How to silence the loudest of our backseat drivers

You are driving down the highway with four kids in the back-seat. Each kid is screaming at you, asking you to do something:

"Go faster!"

"Go slower!"

"Turn left, and I want to eat!"

"Turn right. I want to go to the bathroom."

This keeps happening for the next few hours until you reach your destination. Listening to your backseat drivers will likely cause you to get into an accident. Even if it doesn't, it will leave you stressed, and you may never want to drive with your children as your passengers again.

Our minds have backseat drivers, too. Their screams can be a lot worse than actual backseat drivers. We frequently get into trouble by listening to them and following their instructions.

BACKSEAT DRIVERS OF OUR LIVES

Just as a good drive is a smooth, trouble-free car movement, "happiness is a good flow of life" (Zeno). Just as we can achieve a smooth drive by aligning our driving skills with the rules of the road, we can achieve a good flow of life by using the right reason and aligning it with the way things work (universal reason or *logos*).

Who, then, are our backseat drivers? Who is screaming from behind, making us change course? Stoics identified four of them: *foolishness*, *excess*, *cowardice*, and *injustice*. They called them vices. While we are driving smoothly on the highway of our life, these four backseat screamers distract us, goad us, make us go faster or slower, and make us change course. Because they scream loudly, we listen to them and act on what they demand. As a result, we lose our way, and our life no longer functions smoothly. Let's look at the first backseat driver—folly or foolishness—here.

FOOLISHNESS: THE FIRST BACKSEAT DRIVER

Foolishness is by far the loudest screamer of our backseat drivers. In fact, the remaining three backseat drivers take cues from the first one.

Every minute of every day, things happen around us—people walk past us, someone says something to us, a car speeds up, a child cries, the traffic light changes, and so on. We also experience things that are internal to us—hunger pangs, thirst, and the like. We don't just observe these "impressions" but interpret them as meaning something: A person walking by us is ignoring us, the food we are presented does not taste good, and so on. Some of these stimuli demand a response. For example, someone does not look where they are going and bumps into us. How do we respond? Do we overlook it? Are we annoyed? Our acts are foolish when we fail to act appropriately. What does it mean to act foolishly? From a practical point of view,

> Foolishness is not knowing what to do and what not to and what does not matter one way or the other.

In other words, we need to:

> know what is good, what is bad, and what is neither
> Based on Diogenes Laertius 7.92; Stobaeus 2.5b1

How can we know what to do and what not to do? Consider situations like this:

> You just lost your job. What should you do, and what should you not do? Should you be angry with your boss or the company you work for? Should you vent your anger at someone else? Should you get depressed?

You can hear your backseat driver screaming: "The stupid company you work for, they don't care for their employees."

Or this:

> Your spouse just said they are about to leave you. What should you do, and what should you not do? Should you be angry with your spouse? Should you vent your anger at someone else? Should you get depressed?

Your backseat driver is screaming: "You gave everything to your spouse. Look what happened! You have the right to be angry."

Or this:

> You are diagnosed with cancer. What should you do, and what should you not do? Should you feel sorry for yourself? Should you regret not taking better care of yourself? Should you feel sorry for yourself?

Your backseat driver is screaming: "Why did I get cancer? Why me? This is unfair!"

AVOIDING FOOLISHNESS

What should we do? Should we take instructions from our backseat driver? How do we decide what is appropriate action and what is not? How can we tell what we should or should not do? The answer to this question relates to the basic tenet of Stoicism:

> Some things in the world are up to us, while others are not.
>
> Epictetus, *Encheiridion* 1

What is up to us? Everything is created by our minds, such as what we desire and try to avoid, our intention to act one way or another, our judgments, and the like.

What is not up to us? Everything not created by our minds, such as our body, our wealth, our reputation, what happens in the world, and the like.

When we fail to distinguish between what we control and what we don't, we act inappropriately, thus foolishly. Suppose you lose your job unexpectedly. You may worry about it and fail to enjoy your dinner and the weekend that follows it. You may fail to act on what you could do following your job loss, such as updating your résumé , calling employment agencies, letting future employers know about your availability, and so on. If we analyze our reactions, we see that we are not acting upon what is up to us (enjoying our dinner, relaxing over the weekend, taking actions that will increase our chances of getting a job) but, rather, acting on (in this case, worrying about) what is not under our control: losing our job. We misjudge the impressions, and this is foolishness.

When our backstreet driver screams and says we should be depressed because we lost our job, we should be angry because our spouse is leaving us, or feel self-pity because of a medical diagnosis, if we follow the advice of our backstreet driver, we are being foolish. Why? Because we are trying to control what is not under our control. Being depressed will not bring back our job. Being angry will not make our spouse change their mind. Self-pity will not cure cancer.

WHAT HAPPENS WHEN YOU LISTEN TO YOUR BACKSEAT DRIVER?

What happens when you listen to your backseat driver and act foolishly? You become

> frustrated, pained, and troubled, and you will find fault
> with gods and men.
>
> Epictetus, *Encheiridion* 1

If you refuse to listen to your backstreet driver and act only on what you can control rather than what you cannot,

> No one will ever put pressure on you; no one will impede you; you will not reproach anyone; you will not blame anyone; you will not do a single thing reluctantly; no one will harm you, and you will have no enemy because nothing harmful will happen to you.
>
> Epictetus, *Encheiridion* 1

And the penalty for continuing to be foolish by trying to control what we cannot while neglecting to act on what is under our control? Again, according to Epictetus, there's no penalty. But you will continue

> to be just the way you are: miserable when alone and unhappy when with others.
>
> Epictetus, *Encheiridion* 12

IGNORING THE BACKSEAT DRIVER

Because foolishness is the loudest of our backseat screamers, we need to learn how to ignore it. The remaining three screamers are related to this one. Just by silencing this screamer, we can get rid of most worries about the past and anxieties about the future. And yet, getting rid of anxieties and worries is not enough. After all, psychopaths and sociopaths may not worry about what they have done or be anxious about what they will do. That does not necessarily make them joyful. To be truly joyful, we also need to deal with the other three screamers, which we will talk about in my future posts.

TAKEAWAYS

1. We have four backseat drivers: foolishness, excess, cowardice, and injustice. Their job is to distract us away from a life of happiness.

2. The most distracting of all our backseat drivers is foolishness. Foolishness is not knowing what to do, what not to do, and what doesn't matter.

3. We act foolishly when we try to control things that are not under our control, such as what others think, feel, or do or what happens in the world.

4. We also act potentially foolishly when we don't act on what is in our control.

5. We should ignore the foolish backseat driver. Instead, when something happens that negatively affects us, we should ask ourselves the question, "Is what happened under my control?" If the answer is no, then ask, "What *is* under my control?" and choose that action.

TRY THIS SIMPLE EXERCISE

Sit in a quiet place with a pen and paper. Write down everything that you are annoyed about, worried about, or anxious about. Review it to see how many are within your direct control. If everything is within your control, what is there to worry about? If it is not, what is the use of being annoyed, worried, or anxious? It would be foolish to be so.

Decide not to be foolish. Stop worrying about things you don't control. Decide to make the most of what is under your control.

Our four backseat drivers:
2. Excess

How to control our runaway desires

We saw how our first backseat driver can persuade us to make foolish decisions that can destroy our happiness and lead us to anxiety and worry. Now, let us see how our second backseat driver, excess, can lead us to turn a good thing to do into something that is not good. Our backseat driver's screams are like this:

"This feels good. Drive faster!"

"That car just overtook us. Let's overtake that car!"

"Don't bother about the speed limit. It's fun to go at high speed."

If we keep listening to our backseat drivers, we will likely get into an accident or be pulled over by a cop.

MORE OF A GOOD THING IS NOT ALWAYS BETTER

Many of us believe that some things are good and some things are bad. We think in binary terms. For example, health is good, and disease is bad. Killing someone is bad, and saving someone is good. Being angry is bad, and being tranquil is good. We simply assume that, if something is good, more of it should be better. We seldom stop to think that what is good at one level can also be bad at another:

- We eat a piece of chocolate. It feels good. We eat another piece of chocolate. That feels good, too. "Let's have more!" screams the backseat driver. "Why not?" you reply. Before you know it, you have eaten the whole chocolate bar. Now, you are looking for the second one.

- We have a glass of wine. It feels good. We drink another glass of wine. That feels good, too. "This fun. How about another glass?" says the backseat driver. "Yes, why not!" you say. Before you know it, you have managed to drink the whole bottle of wine.

- We make money to buy the necessities of life, such as food and shelter, which makes us feel secure. We make more money to buy things that make our lives even more secure. "Let's get on with this. Let's make a lot of money so we can feel totally secure," says the backseat driver. "That makes sense to me!" you reply and start making more money. Before you know it, you are consumed with acquiring things without having any idea why you are so desperate to acquire more and more things.

In each of these cases, we start with something that is either good or harmless and turn it into something that is less than desirable. Anything carried to an extreme, even if it is good to begin with, can harm us.

This is the problem with our second backseat driver: Excess.

WHAT IS EXCESS?

Excess is our inability to choose wisely. It is not knowing

> what things must be selected, what should be rejected,
> and what is neither.
>
> Stobaeus 450, Book 2, 5b1

When we don't know what to select or what to leave out, we tend to choose things that weigh us down. Excess is related to our wanting more, consuming more, and striving after more. It arises out of our desires.

Desires, in general, are external-oriented—things we cannot give ourselves. We crave things like money, power, prestige, drugs, and alcohol.

WHY "DESIRES OF WANTS" LEAD TO EXCESS

Not all our desires lead to excess. In fact, Seneca (*Moral Letters* 16) distinguished between two kinds of desires: natural wants (desires of needs) and desires of opinions (desires of wants). It is the desires of wants that lead to excess.

All of us have some basic desires, such as the desire for food when hungry, the desire for water when thirsty, and so on. These are desires of needs. When we are thirsty and drink water, thirst goes away; when we are hungry and eat, our hunger goes away. These desires of needs don't lead to excess. They are common, natural, and easy to satisfy. Then there are desires of wants, what Seneca calls desires of opinion. They include the desire for wealth, fame, adulation, and luxury. The problem with the desire of wants is that these desires can be fulfilled only temporarily. There are several reasons for this (what follows below applies to desires of wants).

Desires are insatiable

Even when we get what we want, our desires are not satisfied. Instead, they are fueled. When we have wealth, we want even more of it. When we have power, we want even more of it. The desires are moving targets. There is no natural limit to desire. As Seneca put it:

> Suppose that the property of many millionaires is heaped up in your possession. Assume that fortune carries you far beyond the limits of a private income, decks you with gold, clothes you in purple [...] you will only learn from such things to crave still greater.
>
> Seneca, *Moral Letters* 16

That is the nature of these desires. They cannot be satisfied by feeding them.

> However much you pile up, it will not end desire but only advance it.
>
> Seneca, Consolation to Helvia

So every time you listen to the backseat driver telling you to get more and more, acting on it will only make the backseat driver scream louder and louder.

Desires are relative

We may be perfectly happy with what we have, but if we come across someone who has more, our desire is fueled once again. Since we can always find someone who has more, desires of wants can never be fulfilled. To quote Seneca again:

> No one who views the lot of others is content with their own.
>
> Seneca, *On Anger* 31

When the backseat driver asks you to get more because someone else has more, remember someone else will *always* have more. Listening to your backseat driver is a loser's game.

Desires enslave us

When we desire something deeply, anyone who controls the object of our desire becomes our master. As Epictetus says, we become slaves to those who have the power to grant or thwart our wishes. We may become sycophantic and lose our moral compass.

> When we desire something, the person who can grant us that becomes our master.
>
> Epictetus, *Discourses* 4.1

Again, there is no reason not to enjoy whatever comes our way. A desire becomes a burden only when we believe we *need* it to be happy. When you follow the instructions of your backseat driver, remember it won't set you free; it will enslave you.

As we saw, we cannot get rid of our desires by fulfilling them because the more we feed them, the more they grow. We will be better off if we stop listening to our backseat driver and instead listen to Epictetus:

> You cannot achieve freedom by fulfilling your desires;
> you can only achieve it by eliminating them.
>
> Epictetus, *Discourses* 4.1

AVOIDING EXCESS

When our backseat driver pushes us to get more, consume more, and "enjoy" more, doing so makes us feel good at first. We fail to realize how we are gradually dragged into a life of always wanting and always trying to get more. The life of excess slowly takes over our lives, and we need all this stuff to be happy. However, the truth is that the desire for excess is standing in the way of our living a productive and enjoyable life.

The most important step in understanding excess is to become aware of how what seems normal and harmless can lead to excess. To become gradually aware of the excess we indulge in without realizing it, do the exercises at the end of this chapter. Keep repeating these exercises over several days.

IN OTHER TRADITIONS

It is not just the Stoics who taught us to be wary of excess. It is also a basic teaching in several other traditions. Aristotle emphasized the golden mean; Buddha taught the middle way to his followers. It is exciting to go to the extremes. But eventually, excess leads to a life of dissatisfaction and enslavement.

Should we give up wanting things?

Stoicism does not say, "Don't enjoy your meal, drink or the wealth you may have"; it does not ask us not to make money or enjoy it; it does not ask us to ignore our bodies. Stoicism is not against health, wealth, or other good things in life. We can enjoy all the "good things" in life, even if they are externals, as long as they don't compromise our virtues and as long as we don't start believing that they are essential for our happiness. So, let's stop listening to our backseat driver—excess—and be moderate in what we seek in life.

TAKEAWAYS

1. We tend to believe that, if something is good, more of it is better. Many things that are good in moderation are harmful when we indulge in excess.

2. We should guard against our backseat driver who keeps telling us to crave more of good things.

TRY THESE SIMPLE EXERCISES

Next time you are about to buy something—such as a new dress or an electronic gadget—stop and think. When was the last time you bought something like that? Do you feel the same way about it now as you did then? Will you be as excited about what you are buying now six months from now? If your answer is "no," then you don't really need this. You are just obeying your backseat screamer.

When you are indulging in something that can be potentially harmful—such as overeating or drinking—and tell yourself, "One more will not harm me," try telling yourself, "One less will not harm me either." If you find it difficult to stop, you are just giving in to your backseat driver.

When you go after something (such as promotions or favors), ask yourself how far you are willing to compromise your principles to get what you want. Is it really worth listening to your backseat driver?

When you give up your work–life balance to make more money, ask yourself what your motive is. If making money is a goal in itself, ask yourself, "Is the desire for excess money preventing me from leading the life I want?"

Our four backseat drivers: 3. Cowardice

How to use courage to calm our fears

You are driving along smoothly. Suddenly, you are startled because your backseat screamer shouts, "Watch out! You are too close to the car ahead of you!" You react and jam the brakes, only to realize that your backseat driver overreacted. You are all right for a while, and the backseat driver screams again, "Someone is tailgating you. Step on it!" You immediately try to go faster. Then you notice no one is really tailgating you. The more you listen to your backseat driver, the more likely it is that your driving will be erratic.

What's happening?

Instead of paying attention to our driving, we start paying attention to our backseat driver. Instead of fearing what we should fear (driving improperly), we fear what we shouldn't. This is the nature of our fears, the source of our cowardice.

FEAR AS THE SOURCE OF COWARDICE

Excess pushes us to want everything in sight. Cowardice does the opposite—making us fearful. As a result, we fear what we shouldn't fear and don't fear what we should fear. Fear is not knowing

> what is terrible and we should be afraid of, what is not terrible and we should not be afraid of, and what is neither.
>
> Stobaeus 450, Book 2, 5b1

There are things in life we should be afraid of, and there are other things we should not be afraid of. But our backseat driver randomly cries out, "You are going to get into an accident. Change lanes!" and we obey that. Our backseat driver then cries out, "You can avoid getting stuck if you go fast. Go fast," and we obey that. We are afraid to challenge our backseat driver's fearful reactions to things.

To ignore the backseat driver, we should be clear in our minds about what is terrible that we *should* be afraid of and what is not terrible we *shouldn't* be afraid of.

WHAT WE SHOULDN'T FEAR: THE CARDS WE ARE DEALT

Consider thoughts like these that pass through our minds:

I am worried about getting old.

I am afraid to die.

I am concerned about getting into an accident.

It would be terrible if I lost my job.

I am concerned about developing health problems.

My coworker is working against me.

This might ruin my reputation.

Our backseat driver is urging us to be afraid of all such things. Which ones should we consider terrible and be afraid of? According to the Stoics, none of these is terrible, and we should not fear them. Why? Because they are externals and, therefore, beyond our control. External things that are beyond our control are nothing to us. We should not fear them because we have no role in creating them, and we can do nothing about them. These are the givens of our lives when they happen to us. They are cards dealt to us in the poker game of life. Our job is not to fear them but to use them to win. If we fear them, we are defeated before the game starts.

A good player does not go into a game fearing what they might have to face. Rather, they get into the game expecting to win with their skill, no matter what is handed to them. If they are fearful of what is handed to them, they are likely to lose the game.

Epictetus was born a slave but was freed. The emperor threw him out of Rome, and he went to Greece to teach Stoicism there. What happened did not matter to him. He always found a way not to be defeated by it.

The same is true of life. If we keep fearing what might happen in the future, even though we can do nothing about it, we will not be effective when we face it. Our focus will be on our fear rather than how to deal with what is in front of us.

When the backseat driver screams, "Watch out, danger!" let's pause for a minute and ask ourselves, "Is it within my power to stop the thing that I am supposed to be afraid of?" If the answer is no, there is nothing to fear because you can do nothing about it.

But what if it happens? Listen to our favorite emperor:

> Do not disturb yourself by picturing your life as a whole; do not assemble in your mind the many and various troubles which have come to you in the past and will come again in the future, but ask yourself, in each present circumstance, what is there in this that is unendurable and beyond bearing? For you will be ashamed to confess. Next, remember that neither the future nor the past pains you, but only the present.
>
> Marcus Aurelius, *Meditations* 8.36

Why are we so concerned about the future? It is mostly because we think that, unless we worry about it constantly, we won't be able to cope with it later. We don't realize we have been dealing with unexpected situations all our lives. We can cope with whatever comes our way.

> Never let the future disturb you. You will meet it, if you have to, with the same weapons of reason which today arm you against the present.
>
> Marcus Aurelius, *Meditations* 7.8

Never fear what may happen in the future if you can do nothing about it now. Seneca goes a step further:

> Others may say perhaps the worst will not happen. You yourself must say. Well, what if it does happen? Let us see who wins!
>
> Seneca, *Moral Letters* 26

When you apply this rule, you will see most of your fears disappear.

WHAT WE SHOULD FEAR: HOW WE PLAY THE CARDS

When you play poker, your success depends much less on the cards you're dealt than on the way you play. A good hand played badly can lose, and a bad hand played well can win. In life, our character is revealed by how we play our cards.

What matters in life is not what happens to us but how we respond to it, our judgments. Judging things correctly is under our control, and we should be concerned about our misjudgments: how we judge impressions. Are our judgments in accordance with reason, or do we go with our first impressions without examining them? Our misjudgments can cause us to harm others. Even more importantly, they can harm us. So we should consider them terrible and fear them. In every fearful situation, you should ask yourself: "Is my judgment on this the right one? Is there another way of looking at it?"

Here is an example. Let the situation be one where you can control your response. Suppose a friend says something casually to you that hurts your feelings. You feel she is harboring an unspoken resentment against you, and your friendship is at risk. This is your impression. If you accept that impression as true, your fear will grow. Your fear probably turns into anger, and you will say something to her, which will make the situation worse. This can disturb your and your friend's tranquility. Now, both will be upset with each other.

Instead, suppose you pause for a minute and examine your impression. Is your impression correct? Is it the only way to look at it? Consider some alternatives.

- Your friend was careless in her remarks. She wasn't trying to insult you.

- Your friend had a lot of things on her mind and wasn't paying much attention to what she was saying.

- She did say something negative, but that was in response to what you said earlier.

- She did say something to hurt you, but haven't you said things that hurt others? Isn't it better to let it go than to escalate the situation?

You will see that getting afraid and becoming fearful of the consequences is only one of the many choices you have in front of you. When you react thoughtlessly to a situation, you are taking instructions from your backseat driver.

DO YOU FEAR THE RIGHT THINGS?

So, what we should not fear in life is what happens to us. What we should fear is our weakness of character in responding to it properly.

In reality, most of us do the opposite. We are afraid of things that we don't control and, therefore, are nothing to us—such as illness, death, poverty, losing reputation, and so on. We fail to be afraid of things like judging our impressions properly, which are under our control. We lose the fearlessness that comes from controlling what is under our control and become fearful of things that we cannot possibly control. We let our backseat driver control us. As Epictetus says:

> What do we fear? Externals. What do we spend our energies on? Externals Is it any wonder that we are in fear and distress?
>
> Epictetus, *Discourses* 2.16

When we realize this, we are not afraid of or averse to anything happening. We are not anxious about tomorrow. We are not worried about what the future may bring. We know anything can happen to us. We cannot control it. But our character and how we respond to things—this we can control. Once we realize this, we give up fearing anything but instead, we spend our time building our character, which will help us face anything that may happen.

TAKEAWAYS

1. There are some things in our life we should fear, and there are other things in life we shouldn't fear.

2. Things we should not fear are externals: what has already happened and what might happen in the future. We can handle them when we face them. We should not be afraid of them since it serves no purpose.

3. We should be afraid of our wrong judgments and how we judge our impressions. These are the building blocks of our character, and we should pay attention to our character and our responses.

TRY THIS SIMPLE EXERCISE

List all things that you are averse to and afraid of—things you don't want in your life now or in the future. Once you have made a complete list, go over the items one by one. How many of the things you are not doing because of cowardice or fear that things won't go your way?

When you identify the items that you are reluctant to do because of cowardice or fear, see that avoiding things because of fear shrinks your world and makes it narrow. If the things you want to do are something you should be doing and are the right things to do, why let fear stand in your way? Your only concern should be whether what you intend to do is the right thing.

Our four backseat drivers: 4. Injustice

How to avoid the trap of injustice

Acting in a just way is a part of living skillfully. But our backseat driver would tell us otherwise:

"What is the big deal? Everyone does that.

"I don't think I need to care what happens to others as long as I am all right."

"Why should I be thankful? I have done so much for her already."

"If I don't grab what doesn't belong to me first, someone else will."

"I know this doesn't belong to me, but I took it only to help someone else."

"It is a "kill or be killed" world out there."

"Sure, it is not mine, but no one will miss it."

There are all forms of injustice. Because acting selfishly results in immediate gratification, our backseat drivers keep encouraging us to act unjustly. And our rewards are immediate. We convince ourselves that, if we are clever, we can escape all the negative consequences of injustice. But injustice is a destructive force in our lives. Let's look at it more closely.

Injustice, the last of our backseat drivers, is ignorance of what belongs to whom. More specifically,

> Injustice is the ignorance of how things are to be assigned or distributed.
>
> Based on Stobaeus, 450, Book 2, 5b2

It is not knowing how to give everyone their due, not knowing what should rightly belong to whom. The concept of Stoic justice is broad. It includes our relationship with our family, friends, country, the world, and even the universe. It includes caring, friendship, compassion, duty to the country, and our place in the world and the universe. Thus, when we pollute the planet, we are unjust because we do not assign future generations what they are due. When we lack compassion, we are unjust because we fail to appreciate that we are a part of a larger whole. We fail to see that what is good for others is also good for us.

WHAT DOES STOIC INJUSTICE INCLUDE?

Stoic injustice includes many things, such as:

- *Ingratitude*: When someone does an act of kindness or does us a favor, they deserve our gratitude. When we don't "assign or distribute" gratitude to them, we are being unjust.

- *Dishonesty*: Whenever we act in a way that benefits us at the expense of others, we are unjust because we fail to give what is due to others. When we take what belongs to others, we are being dishonest. This is dishonest and unjust.

Injustice is a kind of blasphemy. Nature designed
rational beings for each other's sake: to help—not
harm—one another, as they deserve. To transgress its
will, then, is to blaspheme against the oldest of the gods.

Marcus Aurelius, *Meditations* 9.1

NOT DOING WHAT WILL BENEFIT OTHERS

We are connected to everything in the universe. Our connection starts with us, our family, society, and the world and
extends to the entire universe (Hierocles). We need to do what
benefits us and what benefits others. Since we are a part of
the universe, our well-being is tied to the well-being of others.
When we are solely focused on ourselves without any concern
for others, we are being unjust.

What is not good for the beehive is not good for the bee.

Marcus Aurelius, *Meditations* 6.54

Because injustice is not knowing how things are to be assigned,
we are also being foolish when we are unjust. Depending on
the context, being unjust can also mean being excessive or cowardly. Our backseat drivers sometimes demand different things
and sometimes cry in unison.

THE STOIC CONCEPT OF INJUSTICE

Epicurus also considered justice as a virtue. However, he saw
justice as a social contract. He saw no meaning in justice unless
it is reciprocal: I won't harm you so that you won't harm me.

> Justice is a social contract: We don't harm others, so others don't harm us. Justice is nothing in itself without such understanding.
>
> Epicurus, *Principal Beliefs* 31–35 (paraphrased)

But this is not Stoic reasoning. *A Stoic would be just if the entire world is not.* For a Stoic, justice is not a social contract but a social reconciliation.

The Stoic sense of justice is independent of the person or object toward which it is directed. Epictetus is quite explicit on this. A student who is estranged from his brother asks for Epictetus' (*Discourses* = 1.12) help with this question: "How about my brother's life?" and is given this response:

> "It is his art of living. But as far as you are concerned, it is as external to you as land, health, and reputation."

Just in case we are left with any doubt on this, Epictetus adds this later in the same discourse:

> "You are released from all accountability to your parents, brothers, property, life, and death."

In Stoicism, we do nothing *specifically* designed to make others happy. At first, this may sound paradoxical. But not so. Stoicism is very clear on this. As Epictetus clarifies:

> No one has the power to hurt us. Only we can hurt ourselves.

By the same logic, we cannot hurt others. Others hurt themselves.

OUR INJUSTICE HURTS US

So the question arises—if our injustice does not harm others, why should we be just? Why not listen to our backstreet driver and take what belongs to others? Why not stop caring for others and do only what benefits us?

Injustice is a burden because it hurts us. When we deny what is due to others, we believe an external will benefit us. But believing an external will benefit us is foolishness. A Stoic is just because the *virtue of justice is an attribute of the Stoic*. All virtues in Stoicism have this purpose: to live life skillfully. (In fact, Chris Gill describes Stoic virtues as "special skills" (in his introduction to Epictetus, *Discourses Fragments, Handbook*, trans. Robin Hard). This is the reason why injustice should be avoided.

The second reason why injustice hurts us is that we are a part of the whole, and when we hurt anyone, we indirectly hurt ourselves.

WHAT ABOUT PUNISHMENT?

In Stoicism, others cannot hurt us; only we can. So, revenge does not make sense to a Stoic. Yet unjust deeds sometimes call for punishment. The Stoic punishment has only one goal: to educate the attacker about their folly.

Suppose someone physically attacks a person. Then, the attacker has done an inappropriate thing by causing the other bodily harm. So, the Stoic punishment would be meted out so that the attacker would not attack again. What about the mental pain of the victim? A Stoic does not recognize mental pain because it is under the victim's control. If you feel mental pain, it is because you choose to do so. You have the power to stop it. Stoic justice would not punish the attacker for any mental distress on the part of the victim. It would only assign a punishment to educate the attacker for acting inappropriately.

TAKEAWAYS

1. Injustice in any of its forms—ingratitude, coveting what doesn't belong to us, being unfair to others, dishonesty, not being kind—hurts us more than it hurts those who are on the receiving end.

2. Therefore, we should avoid being unjust, even if our backseat driver encourages us to do so.

TRY THIS SIMPLE EXERCISE

Recall a time when you could have expressed your gratitude to someone but didn't; recall the times when you were less than honest in your dealings with others; recall the times when you failed to do what was expected of you because it only benefited others and not you; recall a time when you failed to show gratitude to someone who did you a favor and recall a time when you had the opportunity help others, the community, or the planet and did not because you couldn't care enough.

Realize all these are forms of injustice. They diminish you as a person. Resolve to be more just in your dealings.

PART 3
HOW TO DESIGN
A LIFE THAT FLOWS
WELL

SUGGESTIONS FOR LIVING A FLOURISHING LIFE

By now, we know the simple principles of life can yield huge returns. We also know the obstacles we will face along the way and how to handle them. Now, we need to prepare for the journey to a flourishing life and stay the course.

In a world that pays little attention to quality, we start with these questions: How can we act impeccably in any situation, no matter what others do? Can we be impeccable in all that we do? What should we aim for, impeccability or perfection? How long does it take to be impeccable?

We are so preoccupied with our past and so anxious about the future that we fail to appreciate the freshness of each day. In this part, we will talk about the four freedoms we need to achieve to be completely free of the shackles we created for ourselves. Once we are free, we will see the magnificence of our messy lives. We will discuss how not to be distracted by things that entice us along the way.

Then, we will talk about our sense of poverty even when we have plenty, and how our constant discontent distracts us from enjoying the grand life we are given. We will see how we can live a productive life by learning to be content with what we have without constantly craving more.

We will talk about finding joy in our everyday lives and how to be kind to others.

We will conclude this part by finding ways to bring happiness to ourselves by being joyful and bringing happiness to others by being kind.

Being impeccable

How to make your life a work of art

THE ILLUSION OF PERFECTION

Perfectionism paralyzes us. We *almost* complete things but don't finish them because we are unsure if they are perfect. We *stop* ourselves from doing things because we won't be perfect enough. We *postpone* things indefinitely because we are unsure we can do them perfectly. We *demand* perfection from others, and it drives them crazy.

Yet when I hear statements like:

> "Don't expect her to finish anytime soon. She is a perfectionist!"

> "My boss is so demanding because he is such a perfectionist"

> "I wish I could be as perfect as my mentor"

I hear a tinge of admiration. Many of us have been taught to be perfect: to be a perfect son or daughter, a perfect student, a perfect teacher, a perfect employee, a perfect neighbor, or a perfect citizen. Some people spend an enormous amount of time and energy making things "perfect" because being perfect is "good." We were told it is something we should all strive for.

But what is perfection? If we examine it, we will see that our concept of perfection is mostly based on others' opinions. How can we be perfect if others don't think so? We may think that what we did was perfect until someone disagrees. Then, it is not perfect.

Can we really be perfect? You can work out all you want to get a perfect body, but it will lose its beauty and strength as you age. You can do all you want to be a perfect friend to everyone. Yet, someone will find you offensive. You can do all you want to be a perfect spouse, but your spouse may disagree. None of us experience a perfect life—no matter how wealthy we are, no matter how healthy we are, no matter how wise we are, we cannot escape illness, old age, sorrow, humiliation, pain, or death.

Perfection doesn't exist in nature. Things are constantly in flux.

> Consider that before long, you will be nobody and be nowhere, nor will any of the things that you now see or any of those who are now alive exist. Nature's law is that all things change and turn, and pass away, so that in due order different things may come to be.
>
> Marcus Aurelius, *Meditations* 12.21

What perfection can exist in a universe where no sooner than something appears, it disappears? What perfection can we aim for in a kaleidoscopic universe? Which pattern in a constantly turning kaleidoscope can we say is perfect? Can something that has no shelf-life be called perfect?

IS THERE A PERFECT STOIC?

In Stoicism, the Stoic sage is a perfect Stoic. But does a perfect Stoic exist?

> The sage, being perfectly in control of their rational facilities, will always make the right decision and thus is morally perfect. However, the Stoics were realistic—the sage is also as rare as a phoenix (Alexander, *De Fato* 196.24–197.3, Long and Sedley 61N). They recognized that the likelihood of someone reaching sagehood was vanishingly small.
>
> Liz Gloyn, *Classically Inclined*, Sep. 26, 2018

So, Stoic perfectionism is a concept, and the Stoic sagehood is "vanishingly small." For all practical purposes, it doesn't exist. Even Epictetus, who taught in the Golden Age of Stoicism, had not seen a perfect Stoic:

> Show me a Stoic if you have one. Show me a man who is sick and happy, in danger and happy, dying and happy, exiled and happy, in disgrace and happy. Show him to me, for, by the gods, I want to see a Stoic!
>
> Epictetus, *Discourses* 2.19

Perfection is impossible to achieve; it will be swept away if achieved. Now what?

PERFECTION VS. IMPECCABILITY

There is something more desirable than perfection—impeccability. Perfection may be the mark of a sage who doesn't exist, but impeccability is the mark of a *prokopton* (one who is making progress toward wisdom) who does. What is the difference?

Perfection is a finished product. It depends on external evaluation. Your saying something is perfect does not make it so unless others agree. *Impeccability* is a way of life. It depends on internal evaluation. You can be impeccable without anyone's agreement:

- If you write a report which you think is perfect and if others think it is not, then it is not perfect. But if you write a report carefully, check your facts and objectives, and check your language and tone to the best of your ability, then you write impeccably.

- If you think you behaved perfectly at a party and no one else thought so, then you didn't behave perfectly. But if you considered the context of the party, the guests, and the host and behaved appropriately, then you behaved impeccably.

- If you thought your behaviour was perfect because you spoke with firmness while others thought you were rude, your behaviour was not perfect. But if you first considered how your words might affect others and behaved mindfully, then you spoke impeccably.

We set the standard for our impeccability. We take everything relevant into consideration and act. We are fully concerned with our actions and not about others' reactions unless it has something to teach us.

Perfection is driven by how others evaluate it. It is external. Impeccability is driven by how you evaluate. It is internal. A *prokopton* does not try to be perfect but impeccable.

So what do Stoics say about achieving impeccability? Quite a bit, actually.

1. Do what is right

Internal guidelines, values, and ethics drive impeccability. So, we focus on the right actions and do them fully. What others think doesn't matter. Our question is whether we act appropriately, not how it may seem to others.

> It should make no difference to you, as long as you are acting appropriately.
>
> Marcus Aurelius, *Meditations* 6.2

Being impeccable means, no matter what you choose to do, whether meeting a friend or bringing up a child, you do it fully and appropriately. Once you have done it to the best of your ability, you have done it impeccably. You retreat in peace once you have acted impeccably.

2. Do what is appropriate

Impeccable actions should be appropriate actions. How do we ensure that our actions are right and appropriate? Just imagining that our actions are right will not make them so. We may set our own standards, but we should ensure they are the right ones. This means we should ensure that our actions are not unwise, unjust, excessive, or cowardly.

> Let me show you how to do this. Any time you want
> to know what you should go after and what you should

avoid, relate it to your highest good, the purpose of your
life as a whole. Whatever you do should be in harmony
with this. Only when you see your life as a whole are
you in a position to order the details.

Seneca, *Moral Letters* 71

To be impeccable, you should have a philosophy of life. Otherwise, conflicting interests and temporary advantages will pull you in different directions. For example, if your values indicate that tranquility is important, walking away from quibbles that go nowhere would be easier. You won't be conflicted, and your actions will be impeccable concerning your values. For Stoics, wisdom, justice, moderation, and courage are the most important values. Appropriate actions for them are those that will not violate these virtues.

3. Do your best

Impeccability uses internal standards. It does not need external validation or external yardsticks. Only these, and nothing else, really matter when you act impeccably: Have I done the right thing? Have I done my best?

Even if I lack the talent, I will not abandon the effort
on that account [...] Epictetus will not be better than
Socrates. But if I am no worse, I am satisfied. I mean,
I will never be Milo either; nevertheless, I don't neglect
my body. Nor will I be another Croesus—and still, I
don't neglect my property. In short, we do not abandon
any discipline for despair of ever being the best in it.

Epictetus, *Discourses* 1.12

By his own admission, Epictetus was no Socrates. He was neither as athletic as the wrestler Milo nor as rich as the king of Lydia, Croesus. Yet Epictetus did not neglect his body or his property. Epictetus did not aim for the perfection of Socrates, Milo, or Croesus, but he aimed for the impeccability of his actions.

4. Do it fully

An impeccable action is never half-hearted. When you are impeccable, you are not conflicted; you have nowhere to go and nothing to do except what you have in front of you. Impeccability demands that you do it fully, wholeheartedly. Impeccability of action creates a consuming passion for doing what is in front of us fully, as though it is our last act of life.

> Do every act of your life as if it were your last.
>
> Marcus Aurelius, *Meditations* 2.5

We first consider the appropriateness of our actions. Once we are convinced they are appropriate, we immerse ourselves in what we must do.

> First, say to yourself what you would be, and then do what you have to do.
>
> Epictetus, *Discourses* 3.23

Therein lies our impeccability.

IMPECCABILITY AS A WAY OF LIFE

All our actions—whether having dinner, driving a car, meeting a friend, providing for the family, giving to charity, receiving a gift, or deciding to live a life of virtue—can be done impeccably. The nature of the action does not matter, but the intent does. Impeccability does not depend on the outcome as perfection does. Perfection is an outcome; impeccability is a process. An action becomes impeccable when done wholeheartedly and when it is the appropriate action carried out with the right intent. If it can be done at all, a perfect action takes practice. But we can live and act impeccably starting right now. Perfection is a finished product. Impeccability is a way of life. It begins right now with the right intent. It can lead to perfection, but impeccability is complete even when it doesn't.

An impeccable life is well lived, even when it is not perfect.

TAKEAWAYS

1. We have been taught to be perfect. But we can't be perfect if others see us as flawed.

2. So perfection depends on what others think. Instead of being perfect, we can decide to be impeccable.

3. We act impeccably when we do what is right and act appropriately to the best of our ability.

4. If we choose, we can act impeccably all the time and make it our way of life.

TRY THIS SIMPLE EXERCISE

Recall one of your recent actions that left you doubting yourself or feeling uncomfortable. Ask yourself:

- Was it the right thing to do?
- Was it the best I could do?
- Was it appropriate?
- Did I do it fully?

Recall another one of your actions. Ask the same questions. Repeat this a few more times with some of your other actions.

Remember to apply these four criteria to your future actions.

Appreciating the freshness of each day

How does the river of time sweep our worries and anxieties away

I spent a few years in a remote village when I was very young. A river ran by the village. Some villagers would bathe in the river every day. Each villager had their own spot from which to enter the river. Same spot, same person, and the same river, so it seemed to me, and so it seemed to them. So, when I came across these words of a pre-Socratic philosopher many years later, I had to think twice:

> No man ever steps in the same river twice. For it's not the same river, and he's not the same man.
>
> Heraclitus

I had never thought about it that way. It is not the same river as when you entered it today; the water you entered yesterday is long gone. The water you enter today was elsewhere yesterday and will be gone tomorrow. The river you enter today is a different river. How about you? You are not the same person either. You were a day younger yesterday. Maybe you have learned a few things since yesterday, and maybe you have also forgotten a few things.

But why are we talking about a river?

Because what is true of a river is even more true of the river of time.

THE RIVER OF TIME

We all swim, float, or are carried away by the river of time, which changes constantly. How many of us can even remember what we were worried about or anxious about a year ago or a month ago? Most of our worries and anxieties have been swept away by the river of time, even though some of us want to hang on to them forever. Today's anxieties and worries will also be swept away soon. Not just worries and anxieties, but even those with worries and anxieties will be swept away by the river of time.

> The rapidity of time is boundless—and is more evident when one looks back. For though it goes at breakneck speed, it glides by so smoothly that those who are intent on the present moment fail to notice it passing.
>
> Seneca, *Moral Letters* 49

If we take the time to look at today as it is, we will see that it is always fresh. It is our mind that pollutes the freshness of today with the stale problems of yesterday and the imaginary problems of tomorrow. We don't let the freshness of today spread its fragrance into our lives.

Shut off the past! Let the dead past bury its dead [...]
The load of tomorrow, added to that of yesterday, carried
today, makes the strongest falter.

Sir William Osler

Instead of swimming in today's fresh waters, we look for yesterday's stale waters or tomorrow's imaginary waters.

The Stoics had a lot to say about this.

STOICS DEALING WITH THE SWIFTNESS OF CHANGE

When we brood over yesterday's minor insults and troubles, let's stop and think that we are swimming in yesterday's stale waters, ignoring the fresh waters flowing right before us. Soon, even this will be gone. Tomorrow is too late to swim in today's fresh waters.

Time is a river of passing events. Its current is strong.
No sooner is a thing brought to sight than it is swept
away, and something else takes its place, and this too
will be swept away.

Marcus Aurelius, *Meditations* 4.43

We need to swim in the fresh waters of today. We don't have time to lose.

Do not act as if you had ten thousand years to throw
away. Death stands at your elbow. Be good for something while you live and it is in your power.

Marcus Aurelius, *Meditations* 4.17

What should we do as we watch the swiftness of the flow of the river of time? We should not waste more time, but we should avoid yesterday's stale waters or tomorrow's imaginary ones. We should swim through today's fresh waters and count each day as a separate life.

> Begin at once to live, and count each separate day as a separate life
>
> Seneca, *Moral Letters* 101

When we look at the flow of a river, we can see that, from where we stand, some water has already passed us by, and some may pass us by in the future—maybe. This brief present flow is all we have. The river of life is no different.

> Life is divided into three periods—that which has been,
> that which is, and that which will be. Of these,
> the present is short, and the future is doubtful;
> the past is certain.
>
> Seneca, *On the Shortness of Life* 10

There is no need to be overwhelmed by all these. All we need to do is to stay fully focused on the present.

> Don't let your reflection on the whole sweep of life crush
> you. Don't fill your mind with all the bad things that
> might still happen. Stay focused on the present situation
> and ask yourself why it's so unbearable and
> can't be survived.
>
> Epictetus, *Discourses* 2.1

No matter what is troubling us now, it will be all gone and forgotten soon enough. Knowing this, shouldn't we choose to enjoy the freshness of the day?

TAKEAWAYS

1. Things are always in flux. Every day, we get a day older, we learn something new and forget something new. We think we are the same as we were yesterday. But we are constantly changing, and so is the world we live in.

2. When we understand that everything changes all the time, we will see that our worries and anxieties will be gone soon.

3. We may as well enjoy the freshness of every day, knowing, no matter what our troubles are, they will all be swept away soon by the river of time.

TRY THIS SIMPLE EXERCISE

Imagine yourself watching a freshwater river. Look at the water. It is flowing constantly. The water is always new and fresh. So is your life. Every day is a fresh beginning. You don't have to bring yesterday's baggage—your grievances and anxieties—to today. They only pollute the fresh water of your life.

Forget about the dirty water from yesterday or the water that may flow tomorrow. Today, you have this fresh water. It is the beauty of today. And it is the beauty of every day after today. The river of life is always fresh. Let's swim in it and keep it always fresh.

Letting go of life's regrets

How to deal with our "woulda, coulda, shoulda"

Regret is the flip side of anxiety. Anxiety is about what might happen in the future, and regret is about what has already happened in the past. We will deal with anxiety in Part 4, so for now let's talk about regrets.

WHAT ARE REGRETS?

Regrets are about the past. It is saying to yourself that either you should have done something in the past ("I should have taken that job offer," "I should have set my alarm for an earlier time") or shouldn't have done something ("I shouldn't have married so-and-so," "I shouldn't have cut him off"). Colloquially, we summarize regrets as "Woulda, coulda, shoulda." Suppose you hear two people talking like this:

> "I would have been a better basketball player than Michael Jordan."
>
> "You've never played basketball in your life."
>
> "But I could have."

"You are not even tall."

"But I could have been."

You would think they are crazy because the conversation contradicts reality. Yet you can hear people saying things like this all the time:

"I *should* have left home early to catch the flight."

"I *would* have been happier if I had married so-and-so ten years ago."

"I *could* have been the president of my company if I had not been a woman."

"I *would* have been a multimillionaire if I had not sold my Apple stock so soon."

"I *could* have been a Major League player if I had not sprained my foot at the wrong time."

"I *should* have looked after my health when I was younger."

Such statements make no more sense than the ones by the person who would have been a better player than Michael Jordon.

We spend our lives regretting things and how we "woulda, coulda, shoulda" fixed things—by going back in time, of course.

1. Don't throw away the present

What is common to all such thoughts? They are based on the implied belief that we can somehow fix the past by taking what we now believe to be a better course of action. If we, at some level, don't believe that we have control over the past, then we would immediately realize that "woulda, coulda, shoulda" statements are meaningless. You wouldn't, couldn't, or shouldn't; it is too late, impossible, and, therefore, absurd.

Regrets about the past are even more absurd than anxiety about the future. When we are anxious, we may take action, hoping to steer the future in our way, even if it turns out to be ineffective. Regrets about the past are totally meaningless. You cannot change the past, and it is 100 percent out of your control. This is so whether the past is one minute ago or 50 years ago. The vase you broke doesn't care if it is an antique you bought last week or an old worthless piece of porcelain. It is over and done with. Do you want to throw away your present and future to correct something that cannot be corrected or brought back? You might as well wish you had wings or were Superman.

> Regret for time wasted can become a power for good in
> the time that remains if we will only stop the waste and
> the idle, useless regretting.
>
> Seneca, *Moral Letters* 57

When we use up the present to regret the past, we are ruining the present in addition to the past.

2. Don't try to control what you cannot

To regret anything in our life and say that we "would have, should have, could have" doesn't work for another reason: It violates a basic principle of Stoicism, which says:

> Some things are within our power, while others are not.
>
> Epictetus, *Encheiridion* 1

Your past is definitely not under your control. But when we regret what we "would have, should have, could have" done, we act as though there is a way to travel back in time and fix our past. There isn't. As Epictetus warns us:

> If you think you can control things over which you have no control, then you will be hindered and disturbed. You will start complaining and become a fault-finding person.
>
> Epictetus, *Encheiridion* 1

If we act as though these things are under our control, we not only waste our time but also become fault-finding people, always complaining about something. So, the next time you are tempted to say that you "would have, should have, could have," done something, realize that you don't have a rewind button that would let you go back in time to redo the past. Regrets waste our time without giving us anything in return.

3. You did the best you could

If you regret the past and think you "could have" done better if you had taken another course of action, know you couldn't have taken any other course of action. Why? According to ancient Stoic philosophers, whatever happened in the past was destined to happen.

> Nothing happens at random, but everything for a reason and by necessity.
>
> Chrysippus

If you are uncomfortable with this deterministic approach to life, you may want to look at it differently. When you take any action, you think that's the best course of action you could take, given your knowledge, mental state, and decision-making capabilities at that time. If you could have taken a better course of action, you would have. So whether you believe you had a choice or not, the course of action was the only one open to you at the time of taking the action. Other alternatives were closed to you because of the limitations that existed at that time. There is no point blaming yourself for it now.

4. When something changes, everything changes

Let's say you express a regret like "I should have accepted the other job that was offered to me two years ago. If I had, it would have been much better for my career." Even if it were true, you are assuming that the job you failed to accept has only one consequence: furthering your career. But life isn't like that. When one thing changes, hundreds of other things we never thought of also change. For example, the other workplace might have been toxic, affecting your mental health. You might have met different people in that workplace, changing your social life. That job might have required you to travel too frequently, leaving you no time for your personal life. Many things like this, taken together, might have steered your life differently in unpredictable ways.

Most of our major regrets are based on the misunderstanding that when we change one thing in our lives, everything will remain the same. This is never true. So, again, regret is meaningless because we don't even know how our lives would have turned out if we had actually taken the alternative course of action.

Things are interwoven. When we change one thing, we change many things along with it. Things have both intended and unintended consequences.

> Think of the bond that unites everything in the universe. They are all dependent on one another. All are interconnected and in sympathy with one another.

Marcus Aurelius, *Meditations* 7.38

IF ALL ELSE FAILS, TRY THIS

If none of the above suggestions work for you, try this. Imagine that you have already died. Now, there is nothing to regret because your past doesn't exist anymore. You are a new person. Decide to live properly from this day forward.

> Think of yourself as dead. You have lived your life. Now take what's left and live it properly.

Marcus Aurelius, *Meditations* 7.56

You can't say anymore that you should or should not have done something because your past has magically disappeared. You are now regret-free. How do you plan to live the rest of your life?

TAKEAWAYS

1. We constantly think that we should have done something else other than what we did. These are meaningless regrets since there is no way we can go back to the past and change it.

2. By regretting our past actions:

   a. we throw away the present moment.

   b. we try to change what cannot be changed.

3. We couldn't have done anything differently in the past because we did the best we could.

4. We don't know how things would have turned out if we had acted differently.

TRY THIS EXERCISE

Make a list of things you regret in your life.

Look at them one by one. Do you say to yourself, "I should have done things differently" or "I wish this hadn't happened"?

Realize the meaninglessness of such thoughts. You cannot go back to the past and fix it.

Whenever you catch yourself thinking what you "woulda, coulda, shoulda" done, get back to the present. What you did was the best you could do at that time. There is no use in trying to change what cannot be changed.

Making it easy: run the short way

Get rid of your stories and make your life easy

We tend to complicate our lives. Life gives us simple challenges, and we convert them into serious obstacles. As time goes by, we perfect this art of seeing problems everywhere. When we read what Zeno says—*happiness is a smooth flow of life*—we think, "Wouldn't it be nice to have a life like that? But that is not going to happen with all my problems!"

HOW WE MULTIPLY OUR PROBLEMS

How do we convert simple challenges into insurmountable problems? Through a lot of practice! Our culture (it doesn't matter which one) teaches us to write stories about our experiences, no matter how trivial. Let's see how we casually double our problems:

- Your boss says he wants the report a day earlier. You don't see a request. You write the story in your mind: "My boss is so disorganized. He says something, and then he says something else." *You had one problem before: writing your report faster; now you have two:*

writing the report faster and emotionally coping with your boss's disorganization.

- Your spouse buys something extravagant that you, as a family, can't afford. You write the story in your mind: "My partner is so clueless and so selfish, with no idea of what we can afford and what we cannot." *You had one problem before: your spouse's extravagance; now you have two: your spouse's extravagance and her selfishness.*

- You are driving. Someone cuts in dangerously in front of you. Fortunately, there is no accident. But you cannot keep from getting agitated about the crazy guy in front of you whose dangerous behaviour could have killed you. *You had one problem before: you could have been killed; now you have two: you could have been killed, and you have mental agitation for hours.*

If we look back at our problems, we will see that the second problem we create ourselves through our stories is much more damaging to us than what actually happened. It is also much more persistent and harmful to our tranquility. The harm caused by reality is only a tiny fraction of the harm we cause ourselves by our stories.

FOLLOW NATURE

Stoics follow nature. What do we see in nature?

A hungry child eats. She is not complaining about the bad food yesterday and possible future food scarcity tomorrow. An animal in danger runs. Once it escapes the danger, it goes about its business as usual, not analyzing why it was in danger. The sea becomes calm after a storm. Once the storm has passed, the sea is as calm as it was before the storm. A willow bends when there is a strong wind. Then, the willow straightens.

That is nature's way: respond to things that happen. Nature does not respond to events that are not present or spin stories around them. Only humans do that. Here are some Stoic suggestions.

1. Run the short way

Speak simply. Say what you mean. Act simply. Don't make things complicated.

> Run the short way. The short way is the way of nature.
> Perfecting the soundness of each word and deed is the
> goal. Follow that, and you will be free of anxiety and
> stress, compromise, and pretension.
>
> Marcus Aurelius, *Meditations* 4.51

Look at nature. It acts simply. Water flows, and fire burns. Dogs bark, and cats meow. Birds fly, and fish swim—it's all simple. Nature does not make things complicated, and neither should you.

Avoid problems by acting simply.

2. Focus on the quality of your speech and action

When we say or do something, we elaborate and exaggerate, trying to make it elaborate or ornamental. We try to compensate for the shallowness of our thoughts by hiding behind words. It is best to say what we mean and do what we intend to, without unnecessary exaggerations and elaborations.

It is quality rather than quantity that matters.

Seneca, *Moral Letters* 45

When our minds are clear, and our judgments sound, we say and do everything in the soundest way possible without trying to impress others with our cleverness. When our purpose is clear, we are free from fatigue, hesitation, devious motives, and showing off.

Pay attention to what you say and do. Choose your words so you are clear and do not offend others. Sound words and actions will free you from anxiety, stress, compromise, and pretension.

Avoid problems by the quality of your speech and actions.

3. Look for solutions

When we face a problem, we tend to look for more problems rather than solve the one at hand. We don't look for a solution when something "bad" happens to us. Instead, we say, "Why me?" and go into a self-pity mode. Or we beat ourselves up because we failed to do something that led to this. It is like fighting a fire with gas rather than water. It doesn't solve the problem but only makes it worse.

Strangely enough, the solutions are readily available to us in many situations. We simply overlook them because we are busy finding more problems.

Is the cucumber bitter? Throw it out. Are their briars in your path? Go around them. That's enough. Don't add, "Why are such things in the world?"

Marcus Aurelius, *Mediations* 8.50

When faced with a problem, look for solutions, not for more problems.

4. Don't overlook the resources you already have

When we don't look for solutions, we don't recognize them even when they are right in front of us. Solving problems takes less time than complaining about them. Epictetus mocks us for our tendency to feel helpless when faced with problems:

"But my nose is running!" What do you have hands for, idiot, if not to wipe it? "But how is it right that there be running noses in the first place?" Instead of thinking up protests, wouldn't it be easier just to wipe your nose?

Epictetus, *Discourses* 1.6

When faced with a problem, don't overlook the resources available to you to solve it.

5. Take things as they come

One of the reasons we don't solve our problems in the simplest way possible is that we try to eliminate the "root cause" of the problems instead of dealing with what is in front of us right now. It is reasonable to try to understand the "root cause" of a problem. However, when we face a problem, it makes more sense to look for a solution than to spend our energies finding a solution to all such problems once and for all. Doing so takes the mind away from finding a solution to this problem right now. We move away from:

> taking things as they come and enjoying what is good in each present moment.
>
> Seneca, *Moral Letters* 17

When you face a simple problem, don't make it difficult to solve by enlarging its scope.

TAKEAWAYS

1. We spend more time and energy than needed on life's problems.

2. But it is not nature's way. Nature acts in the quickest possible way and through the shortest way.

3. To act like nature:

   a. Run the short way. Don't complicate things.

   b. Focus on quality.

   c. Look for solutions rather than worrying about the problem.

4. Have clarity on what is right in front of you and what needs your attention.

TRY THIS SIMPLE EXERCISE

Think of three problems you might have faced in the past, preferably recently. How much time and energy did you spend on each? Did the problem demand so much of your energy? Could you have resolved it faster and better?

Can you think of any problems of the past that you could have solved more simply?

Whenever you face a problem in the future, and you feel it will take a long time to solve it, think of a way by which you could solve it better and faster. If you cannot, think of someone you know and admire who gets things done faster and better. How would that person handle it?

Gaining our four freedoms

Looking at the traps we are caught in and setting ourselves free

What is freedom? It depends on who is answering the question. If you are living in an oppressive country, you may say freedom is to be free from oppression. If you are dirt poor, you may say freedom is not worrying about where your next meal is going to come from. If you are a chronically sick person beset with pain, you may say freedom is a healthy body without pain. Depending on who you ask, freedom could be a lot of money, having whatever you want, or having power over others. Or something else.

You have got it all wrong, said the Stoics. Freedom doesn't come from getting rid of the things that afflict us or getting what we are after. Even if you could get rid of what is afflicting you now, there is no guarantee that something else that is equally bad won't take its place. Even if you get all you are after, there is no guarantee that you will never lose it all. True freedom, the Stoics said, is psychological freedom.

> Freedom is not owned by those who bought or sold it.
> It is something you ask of yourself and give yourself.
>
> Seneca, *Moral Letters* 80

It is the freedom that cannot be taken away from you by dictators, poverty, or illness. It is the ability to be free despite what you have or don't have.

Free people are not waiting for someone to grant their freedom and happiness. No matter what condition they find themselves in, they are free. You are free when you realize that no external things can give you enduring freedom, and the only way to realize it is to seek it within. There are four common reasons (arbitrarily classified by me) why we are not free. Let's look at these more closely.

1. Mental freedom: worries and anxieties

When we worry, we are caught up in the past. When we are anxious, we are caught up in the future. We cannot be free when trapped in the past or the future. Worries and anxieties are caused by our tendency to try to control what is not under our control. Neither our past nor our future is under our control.

> Whenever I see a person suffering from anxiety, I think, well, what can he expect? Unless you want something not under your control, how can you be anxious?
>
> Epictetus, *Discourses* 2.13.

You don't have to worry or be anxious, says Marcus Aurelius. And you don't have to wait long. You can let go of the past and the future and have all you have been working toward right now.

> You have been trying to reach many things by taking the long way around. All these things can be yours right now

138

if you stop denying them to yourself. All you have to do is
let go of the past and trust the future to providence.

Marcus Aurelius, *Meditations* 12.1.

And Seneca points to the absurdity of being unhappy before
the things we are anxious about happen. We anticipate sorrow
and experience misery now when we can be happy and free.

What I advise you to do is not to be unhappy before the
crisis comes; since it may be that the dangers before which
you feared as if they were threatening you, will never come
upon you; they certainly have not yet come. Accordingly,
some things torment us more than they should; some
torment us before they should; and some torment us when
they should not torment us at all. We are in the habit of
exaggerating, or imagining, or anticipating, sorrow.

Seneca, *Moral Letters* 13

We don't control the past—it has already happened. We don't
control the future—it is not predictable. So, the right path to
freedom is not to be excessively concerned about these things but
to confine ourselves to doing what is under our control today.

2. Physical freedom: sickness and death

The thoughts that we should always be healthy and never die are
irrational beliefs and not consistent with reality. We can deal with
this in two ways. First, we must realize that sickness and death are
inevitable and, therefore, not under our control. Second, because
these are not under our control, we should accept them and not
be afraid. Here is Epictetus in conversation with a student:

"Do you mean to say that you are immune from illness,
death, age, and disease?"

"No, but I would die and bear disease God-like. This
much is in my power. This I can do. All other things you
say are not in my power, and I cannot do them. I will
show you the strength of a philosopher."

"What kind of strength are you talking about?"

"A desire that is always fulfilled. An aversion that does
not face what it wants to avoid. The right choice. A
well-considered assent. This is what you shall see."

Epictetus, *Discourses* 2.9

What is Epictetus talking about here? He is just saying that you
can do nothing about death or terminal illness, so accept it with
dignity. Be godlike when facing disease or death. This is under
your control. Your only other alternative is to be miserable.

3. Social freedom: what others think

This is a big one. From "What will the neighbours think?" to
irrational demands like "Everyone should respect me," this
self-imposed trap makes many of us unfree. The clothes we
wear, the houses we live in, the cars we drive, the places we
go to, the words we use, and the emotions we display are all
influenced by what others think. It is not always bad to consider "what others may think." We live in a society, and there is
nothing wrong with being adjusted to it. But when we depend
on other people's approval for everything we do, we give up our
freedom. Such fear of public opinion may also show up as anxiety and make us unable to act effectively. Epictetus explains
this well:

> [A] musician when singing by himself has no anxiety,
> but when he enters the theatre, he is anxious even if he
> has a good voice and plays his instrument well; because
> not only does he wish to sing well, but also to be liked
> by the crown: but this isn't in his power.

Epictetus, *Discourses* 2.13

So, to be free, we need to free ourselves from being concerned about what others might think about us unless we are doing something offensive to others. Not bothering about public opinion will carry us a long way to total freedom.

4. Thought freedom: what we think

When we are unhappy because someone else has what we don't have or has more of what we have, we fall into the trap of envy. Envy is often a part of our decision not to be free, even when we have everything we need to be free. We may be happy with the salary raise until we learn that a colleague got a higher increase. Now we are unhappy. The same raise that made us happy yesterday makes us unhappy today. This is an error in your thought process, and it is a very common one. It can be about your house, job, accomplishments, or anything else. Our happiness is not decided by what we have but by what others have. What others have is not under our control; thus, we are trapped. Our judgment that someone else should not have more than us took away our freedom. Since someone else will likely always have more, resentment is a quick way to lose our freedom. Our envy does not affect the person envied. It only deprives us of our freedom. We inflict this on ourselves, and we can choose not to.

Another way to look at it is to realize that you have something the other person does not.

> When you see someone in power, compare it to the benefit you have by not wanting it. When you see someone rich, see what you have instead of riches[…] If you have the advantage of not needing riches, know that you have something more than what the other person has, and that is of far greater value. Someone has an attractive spouse; you, the happiness of not desiring one.
>
> Epictetus, *Discourses* 4.9

GETTING OUT OF ANY TRAP

Here, we covered four major ways of being trapped and losing freedom. But if we look more closely, no matter the problem, the causes and solutions are the same. The structure of all our problems is the same, no matter where they arise or when they arise.

- *We have an irrational belief.* (For example, my past and future should be under my control, others should not have more than me, others should always think well of me, and I should never get sick.) These beliefs are irrational because they are not under our control.

- *We think we can control things by controlling what is not under our control.* (For example, we cannot change our past, change everyone's thinking, or live forever.)

- *We think that, once we change the externals, we will be free.* (For example, we think we will be free if we have more money, prestige, and the like.) Externals don't have the power to set us free.

So the only way to be totally free is to identify the irrational beliefs that underlie our thinking, realize that we are trying to control what cannot be controlled by manipulating the externals, and fully know that externals can never lead us to freedom. Once we fully comprehend this, we will fully focus on what is under our control. When you only deal with what is under your control, you are totally free, and no one can take this freedom from you.

TAKEAWAYS

There are four freedoms that are essential for us to achieve:

1. Mental freedom: freedom from worries and anxieties
2. Physical freedom: freedom from preoccupation with sickness and death
3. Social freedom: freedom from other people's opinions
4. Thought freedom: freedom from our thoughts that are not true.

TRY THIS SIMPLE EXERCISE

Try to think of a problem that has been bothering you. Why do you have this problem? Why aren't you free of it?

Now check to see which of the four freedoms you think you lack to cope with this problem. Think of ways in which you can develop this freedom.

Continue doing this with all your problems. See for yourself how not developing these four freedoms impedes your life. Make a conscious effort to develop these freedoms.

Enjoying the magnificence of our messy lives

How to appreciate the grandeur of everyday life

THE MESSY AND MAGNIFICENT

If you ever feel that your life is not going well, lacks excitement, or is beset with problems and you wish for a different life, let me tell you a story:

> Let's say you have many problems in life—health problems, money issues, and relationship difficulties, to name a few. The sameness of life bores you. You despair of this life and cry out, "God, I can't cope. Get me out of this!" God appears before you and says:
>
> "As you wish. What would you like instead of this life?"
>
> "I want all my problems to go away. I want all wishes to come true immediately. I want everyone to respect me. I don't want to face any trouble from now on."
>
> "Granted. Your problems are all gone."
>
> Your life changes right away. As you had wished, you go to bed on the most luxurious bed you have ever slept on with a beautiful partner. You wake up to a pleasant sunny

morning, to the sound of chirping birds and the aroma of a wonderfully prepared breakfast.

After breakfast, you think, "It's a nice day; let me go for a drive." Your attendant says, "If you would like to go for a drive, your favorite Lamborghini is parked right outside." You take the car for a drive. The highway is clear, and you hit the pedal to the bottom—it's thrilling.

When you come back, your personal chef has a delicious lunch waiting for you. You have your lunch, relax a bit, and doze off. Around mid-afternoon, you feel like swimming in the pristine river you saw when you went for a drive. Your chauffeur appears and says that he is ready to drive you to the river for a swim. You swim in the clearest water you ever saw.

When you return home, your friends visit you. They all admire and respect you. You have an exquisite dinner in their company with your favorite music playing in the background. You go for a walk and then go to bed and sleep like a baby. You feel life couldn't be any better. This is a lot better than you ever imagined.

You enjoy this dream life for a few months, and then it hits you: This is excruciatingly boring. Without any challenges, life is tedious, dull, and miserable. You cannot live this new life much longer without going out of your mind. You despair of your new life and cry out, "God, I can't cope. Get me out of this!" God appears before you and says,

"What do you want now?"

"Anything, God. Anything but this problem-free life that I wished for."

"Granted. Your problems are all back."

You wake up to find you are back in your old life with all its problems. Now, how do you feel about your life? Do you really want to give up the magnificence of this messy life for a problem-free, meaningless existence?

> For if there is a sin against life, it consists perhaps not so much in despairing of life as in hoping for another life and in eluding the implacable grandeur of this life.
>
> Albert Camus, *Summer in Algiers*

The "implacable grandeur of this life" is rooted in the messiness of our daily lives.

The messiness of our lives is the price we pay to experience the magnificence of our lives. Let's not close our eyes because of the price of admission.

It is not that we don't already know this. It is all around us: Pain precedes childbirth. Sore muscles precede a strong body. Sweat precedes a winning goal. Blisters accompany a long hike to the summit. Years of tough discipline precede winning major games. Challenges precede mastery. We pay for every good thing in life. Yet, when it comes to life in general, we fail to understand that messiness is the price of magnificence.

The Stoics were aware of the magnificence of our everyday existence and offered several suggestions for enhancing our awareness.

1. Life is a magnificent festival

The Stoic view is that life is a festival, and we are here to enjoy it.

> As one who would live here in the flesh for a while,
> witness his [God's or Nature's] grand design, and share
> briefly the pageant and the festival with him. So why not
> enjoy the feast and pageant while you are able?
>
> Epictetus, *Discourses* 4.1

We fail to understand the source of our problems. Our fears are meaningless, and our anxieties and worries are of our own making.

You have the resources to cope with any problem. Your lack of this knowledge is the source of your difficulties. Once you realize your happiness is under your control, irrespective of your circumstances, you will have no reason to despair.

2. We can handle our messy lives

No matter how healthy, wealthy, or wise we are, we will face problems in life. The good news is that we can face our problems, no matter what. Most problems lose their hold on you as time passes. If I ask you the three most pressing problems you faced a year ago, I suspect you won't be able to tell me. Yet, it is hard to believe that the problems that bother us now will be gone soon enough. All we need to do is temporarily endure.

> Nothing can happen to you that you cannot endure.
>
> Marcus Aurelius, *Meditations* 5.18

Marcus Aurelius was fighting wars that he would rather not, but that did not stop him from doing his duty and writing his thoughts that inspire us today. Epictetus was lame and an exile, but that did not stop him from teaching. Seneca was exiled, but he became one of the most famous people of his time. They did not think they couldn't handle whatever happened to them. By their will, they became bigger than their problems. We can do the same.

3. Our lack of confidence creates the mess

We often feel our problems are too big to handle. The bigger we think our problems are, the less confident we are. But it is the other way around. As we feel less and less confident, the problems get bigger and bigger. Our lack of confidence makes it difficult for us to deal with them.

> Our lack of confidence doesn't come from difficulty; the difficulty comes from our lack of confidence.
>
> Seneca, *Moral Letters* 21

So, first of all, we should be confident that we are big enough to handle the messiness of our lives. If we aren't, we will be beaten even before we enter the race.

4. We have the resources to fix any mess

But why do we lack confidence? Why do we think we cannot handle the messiness of life? It's because we don't understand that we already have all the resources to cope with life's problems.

> Remember that for every challenge you face, you have the resources within you to cope with that challenge. If you are inappropriately attracted to someone, you will

find you have the resource of self-restraint. When you have pain, you have the resource of endurance. When you are insulted, you have the resource of patience. If you start thinking along these lines, soon you will find that you don't have a single challenge for which you don't have the resources to cope.

Epictetus, *Encheiridion* 10

All we need to do is realize that life is a festival and there's no problem we cannot handle. We feel helpless because we fail to realize that we have been equipped with all the resources to cope with any problems that may arise.

We never need to despair over the messiness of our lives once we see its magnificence.

TAKEAWAYS

1. Our lives are messy. Things don't go as planned, people don't do what we expect them to, things that worked once don't work anymore, and our well-laid plans go astray. All this messiness hides the magnificence of the lives we are given.

2. To appreciate the magnificence of our lives, we should train ourselves to see that:

   a. Life is a magnificent festival.

   b. We can handle the messiness of our lives.

   c. Our mess is created by our lack of confidence.

   d. We have the resources to fix any mess.

TRY THIS SIMPLE EXERCISE

Close your eyes. Think of any problem you have now (or think will likely happen in the future) and the specific inner resources you have to cope with it.

What would you advise if your friend had the same problem? What inner resources can you identify?

Now, apply that resource to your problem.

Having enough

How to be content with what you have

"NOT ENOUGH" IS THE THEME MUSIC OF MODERN LIVES

Joseph Heller, author of *Catch-22*, one of the greatest novels of the twentieth century, was at a party given by a billionaire on Shelter Island. Kurt Vonnegut, a fellow guest and another famous writer, jokingly asked Heller:

> "Joe, how does it make you feel to know that our host made more money yesterday than you did in your entire life with *Catch-22*?"
>
> "But I've got something that he'll never have."
>
> "What is it that you have that he doesn't, Joe?"
>
> "I have enough."

No matter how much we have, we don't seem to have enough. Discontent haunts us.

We will be happy when we get a job. Or when we get that promotion. Or when we go on holiday. Or when we get married. Or when we get divorced. Or when we have more money.

Or when we retire. Even when we get what we want (as we often do), we feel it is the next thing that will do it. Our happiness is just around the corner, but we are not there yet.

Discontent is not confined to the poor or the obscure. You can find as many discontented people among the rich, famous, and the accomplished. This is true no matter how much we have, how accomplished we are, or how famous we are. No matter what we have, we don't have enough. We are like the billionaire in the above story. Not many of us are like Joseph Heller.

Not having enough is the theme music of our lives—even when we are well-off. This discontent gnawing at our happiness is of such a low level of intensity that we hardly notice it.

WHAT IS ENOUGH?

So, how much money, how many material things, and how many relationships do we need to be content? Not much, says Marcus Aurelius, who ruled the largest empire of his time.

> You need very few things to be happy.
>
> Marcus Aurelius, *Meditations* 7.67

Seneca, probably the wealthiest private citizen of his time, agrees:

> These words are by no means untrue, nor so surprising
> [...] how much we possess that is superfluous; and how
> easily we can make up our minds to do away with things
> whose loss, whenever it is necessary to part with them,
> we do not feel.
>
> Seneca, *Moral Letters* 87

When we begin noticing how many rich and famous people are not content with what they have and how many people who have next to nothing seem to be content even if they have very little, we wonder what makes us content.

Stoicism offers many strategies we can use to move away from discontent to becoming content, to have the feeling of having enough. Let's look at some of these.

1. Separate natural needs from opinion-based wants

Our discontent arises from two types of unfulfilled desires: natural needs and opinion-based wants.

Natural needs are things like food, water, shelter, clothing, and the like. We need food and water to survive. We need shelter and clothing to protect us from the elements. Such needs are easy to fulfill. These needs are temporary, and once they are fulfilled, they go away. When you drink water, your thirst is quenched. When you eat food, your hunger goes away.

Opinion-based wants are things like money, exotic foods, fancy houses and clothes, reputation, prestige, and the like. They can never be fully satisfied because they are opinion-based. These needs are persistent and, once fulfilled, they grow stronger. If you are famous, you want to be more famous. If you become more famous, you want to be even more famous. If you have money, you want more money. If you have more money, you want even more. We constantly strive to reach our goal without ever realizing that our goalpost is always moving and is never reachable. This is how we become obsessed with money, fame, and power. This is how we become gluttons and alcoholics.

> Natural desires are limited, but those which spring from
> false opinions can have no stopping-point. The false has
> no limits. When you are traveling on a road, there must
> be an end; but when astray, your wanderings are limitless.
>
> Seneca, *Moral Letters* 16

So, if you want to be content, learn to separate natural needs, which are easy to satisfy, from opinion-based wants, which continue to fuel discontent. Limit your opinion-based desires.

2. Look at what you have, not what you lack

We have a good job which pays us $100,000 a year. We are happy with it for a while. After a little while, all we notice is that we lack a job that pays us $150,000. We have a million dollars. We want 5 million. Our focus is always on what we don't have and not on what we do have. No matter how little we think we have, right now, there are billions of people around the world who would be excited to have a life like ours: all we can eat, a roof over our heads, no arbitrary punishment, relative freedom and political stability, relative physical safety, access to healthcare, however limited—things like these are beyond the reach of billions of people around the world right now. Yet we are not content. Why? Because we don't look at all the great things we have but only at what we don't have. And what we don't have, we probably can never have because of opinion-based desires with moving goalposts. We don't see how many of the things we now have we would miss if they were taken away from us.

Don't dream about things you don't have. Instead, think
about the best things you now have and how much you
would crave them if you didn't have them.

Marcus Aurelius, *Meditations* 7.27

Epicurus, often (mistakenly) associated with advocating fleeting
pleasures, has this to say:

Anyone who does not think that what they have is more
than ample is an unhappy person, even if they are master
of the whole world.

Epicurus, *Principal Doctrines* 15

3. Don't mistake the treadmill for the racetrack

Your desires seem attractive before you achieve them but lose
their attraction once you do. Do the things you bought last
year, thinking that they would make you happy, make you as
happy now as when you bought them? Or are you thinking
of something else that will make you happy now? There is
no harm in having more, but there is harm in believing your
wants are your needs. You probably have most of the things
you hoped for when you were young. See that, and you will
realize that you are not on a racetrack but on a treadmill.

Fix a limit which you don't want to exceed even if you
could. Get rid of all those dangerous things. They look
better to those who hope for them than to those who have
attained them. Get rid of luxuries that are only for show.

Seneca, *Moral Letters* 15

The only way to be content is not to crave more and more and more but to look at what you have, enjoy it fully, and limit your opinion-based desires.

> Wealth consists not in having great possessions but in having few wants.
>
> Epictetus, *Discourses* 2.2

Most of us already have enough or more than enough. We just need to know it.

TAKEAWAYS

1. No matter how much we have, we tend to look for more things or better things. We never seem to have enough.
2. We crave more because:
   a. We treat our treat our desires like needs.
   b. We fail to look at what we have, only what we think we lack.
   c. We treat our treadmill of desire that does not get us anywhere as though it is a racetrack.
4. When we don't indulge in excess, we can live in content with what we have.

TRY THIS SIMPLE EXERCISE

Think about whether you are happy with what you have. Or do you think you will be happy when you have a bigger house, a better job, more money, or something else?

If you think you need more to be happy, think back to a time several years ago. Perhaps you were a student then. Maybe you thought a good job, a good house, and a partner would make you happy? Maybe you have all of them now? But your list of wants has changed.

Even if all your current desires are fulfilled, realize the you will have a new list soon.

Finding joy in our lives right now

How to find joy in our daily lives

THE JOY OF LIVING

Addressing his friend Lucilius, Seneca says:

> Above all, my dear Lucilius, make this your business:
> learn how to feel joy.
>
> Seneca, *Moral Letters* 23

"Right," you say, "It was easy for Seneca to say that. He was the richest man of his time, and Lucilius was a powerful official. With their money and influence, they could afford anything in life. They already had everything in life, and all they had to do was to 'learn to feel the joy.' But what about me? I am worried about my job security, my shaky personal relationships, my mortgage, my overdrawn credit card, and my migraine. What about me? Where do I find joy?"

Indeed. Where do we find joy?

We intuitively feel that, to be happy, we need money, the respect of others, health, good relationships, and many other things. Our family, our friends, and society in general reinforce this idea. But most things on our list are not under our control but at the mercy of others or of chance. If joy depends on such external things, it cannot be guaranteed because it can always be taken away from us by others or changing circumstances. We can never achieve it unless we solve our long list of problems.

Stoics rejected the idea that joy (happiness or *eudaimonia*) could depend on external factors. Who is happy, then? They argued that you don't need to be healthy, secure, or well thought of to be joyful. You can even be in danger of dying or being deported. They said it is possible to be

> sick and happy, in danger and happy, dying and happy,
> exiled and happy, in disgrace and happy.
>
> Epictetus, *Discourses* 2.19

Epictetus defined a Stoic this way: We should find joy wherever we are, no matter how life treats us. Stoics lived this way. For example, when Seneca was exiled, he did not moan about his misfortune but wrote this to his mother:

> The place which one leaves does not matter; only the
> mind which makes us miserable in our place of exile.
>
> Seneca, *Consolations to Helvia* 10

Nothing that happens to us matters. Externals cannot make us miserable. It's our mind's job to make us miserable or joyful. Yet, it is easier said than done for most of us. Maybe we won't get there today or tomorrow, but the entire Stoic training aims to achieve joy even when our wealth, health, physical freedom, and relationships are snatched away.

We cannot find joy by pursuing it, but we can find it in our everyday lives if we become aware of it. Here are three practical suggestions to become aware of joy's presence in our lives.

1. Finding joy in living: *joie de vivre*

Can we find joy that has nothing to do with our circumstances? The answer is yes, and most of us have experienced it. You may recall getting up in the morning and feeling happy for no reason. You are not happy *because* you have something, you have achieved something, or things are going your way. In fact, such thoughts don't enter your mind at all. You are just happy to be alive. This is what the French call *joie de vivre*.

You can observe this in young children. Before they are taught whether they are poor or rich, fat or thin, respected or despised by others, they are joyous doing what they are doing, playing in a grand mansion in an exclusive give or on the streets in a slum district. Then, society teaches them that they have got it all wrong. They are not supposed to be happy unless they acquire things, and things go their way. They gradually lose their joy of being and learn the joy of having.

Although we gradually start exchanging the joy of living for the joy of having, the joy of living never leaves us. We occasionally continue to experience the joy of living, even briefly. So we know that it is possible to be happy just being alive.

> This world is a mirror of beauty, yet no man sees it.
> It is a temple of majesty, yet no one regards it …
> It is a Paradise of God.
>
> Thomas Traherne, *Centuries of Meditations* 26

2. Finding joy in everyday things

A friend who recently visited the Louvre in France talked about a Cézanne painting depicting a sunrise. Another friend commented that he wished he could afford a holiday in France and visit the Louvre. He sounded deprived.

Yet, although I have been fortunate enough to visit some of the world's best museums, from the Louvre in France to the State Hermitage in Russia, I have yet to see a painting that matches or even comes close to, the brilliance and beauty of an actual sunrise that I can see on any day from my window. The smile on Leonardo da Vinci's *Mona Lisa* is one of the many we can see on people's faces every day. I haven't seen anything as exquisite as a spider weaving its web or a centipede crawling on the floor in any museum. When we see an artist capturing a moment of nature's brilliance, we applaud it. But we fail to appreciate nature itself, of which art is a pale imitation.

Am I romanticizing everyday life? I don't think so. Marcus Aurelius, who ruled the largest empire the world had seen until his time, could have had anything he wished. Yet, what brought him joy was the casual charm of nature.

> We should also remember the casual grace and charm of nature. A loaf of bread splits open in the oven; random cracks appear on it. These unintended flaws are right and sharpen our appetite. Figs, when they ripen, also crack open. Olives, when they are about to fall just before they decay, appear more beautiful. So are drooping stalks of wheat, the wrinkling skin of a staring lion, foam from a wild boar's mouth, and many more such sights.
>
> Marcus Aurelius, *Meditations* 3.1

He continues:

> The grinning jaws of lions and tigers are as admirable as
> paintings or sculptures of them. So is the mature beauty
> of an old man or an old woman and the loveliness of
> children. Things like these will not appeal to everyone,
> but the person who has developed a real friendship with
> nature and her works will be fascinated.
>
> Marcus Aurelius, *Meditations* 3.2

Everyday sights and sounds hold delights that we fail to see. We
rush to see great artists who imitate nature and fail to stop and
look at the far superior original.

3. Finding joy in everyday normal functions

Our everyday normal functions, whether taking a shower or
making breakfast, are delightful and can be a source of joy.
We fail to notice this because, when we shower, we think of
making breakfast, and when we make breakfast, we think of
our work. We cannot find joy by looking for it but by becoming aware of it.

Almost nothing makes happiness harder to reach than trying
to find it. This is powerfully illustrated by the anecdote about
the historian Will Durant, described by June Callwood: Will
Durant searched for happiness in knowledge but only found
disappointment. He looked for it in travel and found tired-
ness, in wealth and found arguments and worry. He sought
happiness in his writing and only felt tired. Then, one day, he
saw a woman waiting in a small car with a sleeping child in her

arms. A man got off a train and came over and gently kissed the woman and then the child, very softly so he wouldn't wake him. The family drove away, and Durant suddenly realized what true happiness is. He relaxed and found that every normal, everyday part of life holds some joy.

Joy is not hidden away from us. It is close to us, within our hand stretch. We can't see it if we close our eyes to it.

> It is not too far from us. We can discover this. All we need to know is where to stretch our hand. But we behave as if we are in the dark and try to reach a place beyond what is closest to us. In doing this, we knock down the very things we want.
>
> Seneca, *On the Happy Life* 3

TAKEAWAYS

Joy is not hidden from us. It is all around us. But we don't find it because we look for it in places where it is not—in money, power, and prestige. We can find joy:

1. by being aware of its presence in our lives
2. by appreciating the joy inherent in everyday things
3. by appreciating the joy inherent in everyday actions

TRY THESE SIMPLE EXERCISES

Exercise 1

How do we get back to the joy of living? Gradually. If we become more and more aware of the truth of Thomas Traherne's words, we can start practicing them.

When you wake up in the morning and open your eyes, remind yourself how beautiful the world is with all its problems. Think of the coordinated way the universe works—day and night, different seasons. Planets moving in predictable paths. Appreciate the beauty of it all.

As you practice this exercise, you will soon realize the inherent joy of living in this world.

Exercise 2

Take the time to look around you. If you see a tree, see it as if you are seeing it for the first time. Look at the trunk. Look at the shape of the leaf. Observe how beautiful they are and how each leaf is unique.

When you see a child, observe their face. See how clear their skin is. Observe other people's faces and see the difference.

Bring the same attention to objects such as lamps, plates, and other things you see. Can you see the beauty that surrounds you?

Exercise 3

When you are in a social situation, observe how people greet each other. See the happiness on their faces. Notice the joy on people's faces in different situations.

Being kind

How to practice kindness

ACTS OF KINDNESS AND RECIPROCITY

When we are good to someone, we expect them to be good to us. When we help someone in need, we expect them to help us when we need help. You scratch my back, and I scratch yours. You invite me to your party, and I invite you to mine. You lend me your tools, and I lend you my lawn mower. This principle of reciprocity is so ingrained in our culture that we can see it everywhere.

How deep-rooted is the idea of reciprocity, which forms the basis of gratitude? A few years ago, a psychology professor decided to send Christmas cards to perfect strangers. To his great surprise (or maybe not), many who received the card responded by sending him a card back, although they had no idea who he was.

And yet, you may have encountered people who don't think that they need to reciprocate. You went out of your way to help someone several times, and now you need a minor favor from them, and they come up with flimsy excuses not to do it. You can't believe it. This person, who accepted your help several times, is now a stranger to you. You were kind to them at the time of their need, and this is how they repay you. You feel cheated and taken advantage of. How can they do this? All your friends share your outrage about such ingratitude. They amplify your outrage with choice epithets like "taker," "deadbeat," "flunky," or "freeloader." Some people are so frustrated by a lack of reciprocity that they feel it is futile to be kind.

How do we deal with people who take our kindness for granted? Maybe we should tell them what we did for them, remind them indirectly, stop being kind to others in the future, and tell others about this.

After you have gone through all such responses mentally, you wonder what would be the best response to such a situation. What would a Stoic do?

1. Start with yourself: Were you really kind?

The best place to start is not with the other person but with yourself. Why did you do favors for the other person? Why were you kind to them? Is it because you wanted to be kind, or were you expecting something in return? If you were "kind" expecting something in return, you were not kind at all. You were in a business transaction that didn't work well for you. Real kindness does not expect anything in return.

> There is no grace in a benefit that sticks to the fingers.
>
> Seneca, *On Benefits* 2.1

Or, as Epictetus put it:

> One who performs a benefit should never remember it.
>
> *Epictetus, Fragments* 40

A truly kind person is kind for the sake of being kind. Being kind for some future benefit is a form of business transaction. It is not kindness. When it is not a business transaction, the question "What's in it for me?" is meaningless. When you feel that some corresponding benefit should come your way, your acts can no longer be considered kind.

2. What about the other person?

Even those who are genuinely kind are sometimes bothered by other people's indifference when they are in need. Remember, just as kindness is something you chose, the other person chose ungratefulness. You cannot really know other people's motives or control other people's behaviour. You only have control over what you think and do, not what anyone else thinks or does.

> You have done a good deed, and someone benefited from it. Why are you, like an idiot, holding out for more—such as applause for your kindness or some favor in return?
>
> Marcus Aurelius, *Meditations* 7.73

You are kind because that is what you choose to be. What the other person chooses to be is their business. Cutting people out who don't reciprocate your kindness makes your world smaller and your motives suspect.

No purpose is served when we wonder why someone is the way they are. We don't wonder why mosquitoes are small and elephants are big. Why should we wonder if some people don't appreciate the benefits they receive? It's the way they are, and it's none of your concern.

3. Should you stop being kind?

Another common response to such behaviour is to cut that person out of your life. You may say, "OK, I don't care if I got anything from my past kindness to this person. But I don't want to have anything to do with him anymore."

This is another way of saying that you would confine your acts of kindness only to those you expect to be kind to you. It also shrinks your world. Kindness is like sunshine. The sun does not shine on you because you are a good person or did something to benefit the sun. It shines on you because it is its nature. If you hate the sun, it will still not hold back its light from you.

> If one were compelled to drop everything that caused trouble, life would soon grow dull amid sluggish idleness.
>
> Seneca, *Moral Letters* 81

We must realize that only what we do counts when we do something to benefit others. How others receive it doesn't concern us.

> As long as you work for the benefit of others, your life is complete.
>
> Marcus Aurelius, *Meditations* 10.5

TAKEAWAYS

When we are kind to others, we expect kindness from them. When we don't get it, we feel offended. This is a mistake.

1. If you are kind and expecting kindness, you are not truly kind because you treat kindness as a business transaction.

2. An act of kindness is complete in itself. It is meaningless to wait for an acknowledgment of your kindness.

3. You should never stop being kind because others don't reciprocate. The purpose of kindness is to benefit others and not benefit yourself.

TRY THIS SIMPLE EXERCISE

One way to practice true kindness without expecting any reward is to work with situations in which rewarding you for your acts of kindness is impossible. Here is how it works:

- Do at least one act of kindness each day.

- The only condition is: if someone finds out about it, the act doesn't count.

By practicing this regularly, you will be kind for the joy of being kind.

PART 4
HOW TO HANDLE EVERYDAY PROBLEMS

BEING PREPARED FOR WHATEVER LIFE THROWS AT US

By now, you should have a good handle on the basic principles, know how to handle the obstacles to your practice of those principles, and know how to design a life that flows smoothly.

But it takes a while for these principles to become second nature to us. Meanwhile, we are faced with many everyday problems, such as:

- How do I stop overthinking?
- How do I deal with insults?
- How do I stop from taking offence?
- How do I get rid of feelings of guilt?
- How do I stop being anxious?
- How do I overcome feeling helpless?
- How do I stop looking for approval from others?

- How do I handle adversity?
- How do I handle ingratitude?
- How do I let go of life's regrets?
- How do I get up when I am knocked down?

We will explore these topics in this section.

Overcoming overthinking

How to avoid overthinking

"BE WATER, MY FRIEND"

Throw a small pebble gently in a still pond. You will see the water forming ripples around the pebble, and soon, the pond will be still again. Throw a large rock with great force. This time, the water forms wider ripples and takes longer to settle. Depending on whether the stone is large or small, whether it hits the water with greater or lesser force, the ripples will form and then settle down. Water never reacts to force any more than necessary.

Most of us are not like water. We overthink and overreact. Someone throws a small pebble in our mental pond, and it creates wide ripples in our minds that never seem to settle. We use enormous mental energy to deal with a simple problem and don't really solve it. All we do is hurt ourselves in the process. It is like using a sledgehammer to swat a fly. We miss the fly and drop the sledgehammer on our foot. Small inconveniences irritate us. Newspaper headlines make us worry too much. TikTok "influencers" may make us want things we didn't even know existed the day before. We take a careless comment by someone as a major insult. We worry for hours about a "negative" comment made by our boss. We are depressed about the injustices that surround us.

Often, it seems there is no way out. Whatever we do results in overthinking. We give money to a homeless person. Immediately, we start thinking, "Maybe he is a drug addict. Or a conman. I shouldn't have given the money to him." The next time, we pass a homeless person without helping him. We start the over-thinking cycle again: "I shouldn't have passed him by without helping him. After all, it would have been easy for me to give him some money." If we buy a dress, we wonder whether it is really necessary. If we don't buy it, we wonder whether we should have. If we buy stuff on sale, we worry about having spent money on things we didn't really need. We feel upset if we don't buy because we passed up an opportunity.

In everything we do, there are endless opportunities to overthink. Most of us immediately take the opportunities and spend our time overthinking. We spend our time unproductively overthinking rather than living a vibrant life.

What can we do about it? Here are four Stoic strategies to over-come overthinking:

1. Draw on your strengths

We overthink because we feel trapped and have no way out. We start to overthink. Our minds go through a stage of self-pity. "Why did this happen to me?" or "I should have handled the situation differently." Essentially, we feel trapped by what happened, and there seems to be no way out. But this is sel-dom true. Instead of thinking such thoughts, if we turn our attention to what we can do about it now, we may find that we didn't lack the strengths; we didn't look for them. Epictetus challenges our helplessness this way:

Have you not received the inner strength to cope with any difficulty that may arise? Have you not been given strength, courage, and patience? Why should you worry about what happens when you are armed with these virtues and have the power to endure? What could constrain, compel, or even annoy you? You don't see all this. Instead, you moan, groan, shed tears, and complain.

Epictetus, *Discourses* 1.6

Finding fault in something and blaming someone for it leads to overthinking. Finding resources to solve our problem makes it go away. If you think you have bought something overpriced, return it rather than overthinking it: "Why are the prices so high?" "I bought something that's not worth the price I paid for it."

Why overthink something when you have the strength to reverse your decision?

2. Look for the solution

Sometimes, we don't even have to look for resources to deal with a situation. The solution is obvious. Yet, we start overthinking by diverting our attention to the problem instead of the solution. Instead of accepting the solution right before us, we go in different directions with an agitated mind.

Is the cucumber bitter? Throw it out. Are their briars in your path? Go around them. That's enough. Don't add, "Why are such things in the world?"

Marcus Aurelius, *Meditations* 8.50

If the restaurant is noisy, go to a quieter one. If things are too pricey, buy them on sale or go to a discount store. There are no satisfactory answers to questions like why a restaurant is noisy or why things are pricey. We can overthink questions like these forever or simply find an alternative and get on with our lives.

Why overthink about something when you can make it go away quickly?

3. Let go of unsolvable problems

You did something, but it went wrong. Now, you can't stop thinking about it. Your job interview did not go well, and now you are going over in your mind the various ways you should have handled your interview. You unintentionally insulted someone, and now you are trying to correct yourself mentally over and over again. A stranger was rude to you, and you can't stop thinking about it. What is common in all such situations? You are overthinking and making yourself miserable without solving any problem because there is no way to solve it.

> If you think you can control things over which you have no control, then you will be hindered and disturbed. You will start complaining and become a fault-finding person.
>
> Epictetus, *Encheiridion* 1

If you are overthinking a situation about which you can do nothing, the only thing this will lead to is more overthinking. You can't get rid of overthinking by overthinking. Anytime you find yourself overthinking about an unsolvable problem, realize that you can't solve the problem by overthinking because you are only feeding it.

Why feed overthinking by overthinking?

4. Don't replay solved problems in your mind

A peculiar tendency of humans is to overthink problems that are no longer present. You were about to get into an accident but didn't. Yet you go through this scene over and over in your mind days after the incident. You even replay your fright at that time. You had a bad childhood. Now you are an adult, and yet you can't stop replaying your childhood long after it's over. You indulge your overthinking. Even animals don't do that.

> Wild animals run from the dangers they actually see, and once they have escaped, they worry no more. We, however, are tormented alike by what is past and what is to come. A number of our blessings do us harm, for memory brings back the agony of fear while foresight brings it on prematurely. No one confines his unhappiness to the present.
>
> Seneca, *Moral Letters* 13

Whenever your mind wanders into watching movies of the past—whether it happened 20 seconds or 20 years ago—and starts overthinking, ask yourself, "It's over. Why am I overthinking instead of being happy that it is over?

Why overthink a problem that doesn't exist anymore?

A RETURN TO STILLNESS

Once you look at your overthinking and see that you have the resources to solve it, or the solution is obvious, not solvable, or already solved, you will see that overthinking is a useless activity and serves no purpose. So, as soon as possible, return to stillness—just like the pond water that returns to stillness after being disturbed.

Be water, my friend.

Bruce Lee

By all means, let's think. But not overthink.

TAKEAWAYS

When we overthink we spend more energy trying to solve a problem that doesn't deserve it. It leads to mental conflict. To avoid overthinking:

1. Draw on your resources to solve the problem quickly.

2. Don't spend time thinking about the problem. Look for quick solutions.

3. Let go of unsolvable problems.

4. Don't replay the problem in your head over and over again.

5. Find a quick solution, solve the problem and move on.

TRY THIS SIMPLE EXERCISE

Next time when you catch yourself overthinking about a problem, ask yourself the following questions:

- Do I want to spend so much energy to solve this problem?

- What is the quickest way to solve the problem? (If you have more than one solution, don't spend time going back and forth between the two. Just decide on one, even if it is not the optimal solution.)

If you find the problem has no real solution, don't turn the problem over and over in your mind. Move on.

Insult? What insult?

How to make insults slide like water off a duck's back

The problem with insults is we can't stop thinking about them. We think of clever comebacks later in the day. We stew over them long after the person who insulted us has forgotten it or even died. It is not uncommon for people to carry around the insults they were subjected to when they were young (and pass them on to others along the way).

Some of us are easily insulted, and others less easily so. What insults us? It depends. Anything can be a source of insult. For example:

A friend passes you without greeting you.

Your boss says that your work is not up to par.

A colleague says, "You don't understand."

Your spouse says, "You are insensitive."

You are passed over for a promotion.

Any of these, and thousands of others, can be sources of insult.

We know it is not worth losing our peace of mind over insults. Our rational mind tells us, "Get over it!" yet we cannot. So we turn to our trusted Stoics and ask them what we should do.

Here's what they will tell us: *We are mistaken, we got it all wrong, we got it backwards*, or *we are taking things too seriously*. Follow the Stoics, and you will see insults will slide over you like water off a duck's back.

1. You are mistaken: It may not be what you think

A new employee, your coworker, passes you without greeting you even though you tried to smile at him. You are insulted and think that he is arrogant or that he thinks he is superior to you. Before plotting your revenge against your coworker, listen to Epictetus:

> Who, then, is invincible? The one who cannot be upset
> by anything outside their reasoned choice.
>
> Epictetus, *Discourses* 1.25

They may not have meant it as an insult. For example, the friend who passed you without greeting you may be preoccupied with something in their life: a serious health diagnosis, an upcoming mortgage renewal at a higher rate she cannot afford, or some other preoccupation. Or the new coworker who doesn't talk to you may not be arrogant. He may just be very shy. Why take these things personally? Always give the benefit of the doubt to the other person and move on.

Besides, not feeling insulted makes you invincible because you are not at the mercy of how others behave (even if you strongly believe that they meant to insult you).

2. You got it all wrong: It is not an insult—it's the truth

What we consider an insult may not be an insult at all. It may be partly or wholly true. For example, your spouse says you don't pay attention to them when they talk. You immediately jump to your defense and explain to them, rather sharply, that you do listen to them. You do so based on your impression that you are a good listener. Pull back a little and take Epictetus' advice:

> Don't let the force of an impression when it first hits you knock you off your feet; just say to it, "Hold on a moment; let me see who you are and what you repre-sent. Let me put you to the test."
>
> Epictetus, *Discourses* 2.18

Calmly consider if it is possible that your spouse could be right—even partially. When your boss says your work is not up to par, maybe it isn't. Think about it. If there is even an element of truth in what they say, thank them and decide to do better the next time. You would have learned something, and your spouse would think you are not that insensitive after all, and your boss would be happy you took her criticism constructively.

Remember, there may always be some truth behind what we think is 100 percent an insult.

3. You got it backward: They are not hurting you— you are letting them

But even after examining your impression, you believe that your impression is correct. You believe you are one of the most sensitive people who ever lived, and the insult is totally unjustified. Other people's opinions do not change who we are. If your name is Jane and someone says your name is John, it doesn't make you John; it just means they are mistaken. If somebody thinks you are a tree, it doesn't make you a tree; it just means that perhaps they may be delusional. In such cases, we recognize that we are what we are, irrespective of what others think. So why should we be upset if someone thinks we are stupid? Why should we spend time thinking about it or being upset about it? If someone has a distorted version of reality, it affects them, not us. We don't become stupid because someone thought so, any more than we become a tree because a deluded person thought so.

> The best course, therefore, is to treat with disdain the injuries which are offered us and to rise above them; to consider that the man who does us an injury is acting according to his nature and to let him be, just as we let a horse kick, a dog bark, and a wild beast attack.
>
> Seneca, *On Anger* 2.32

Also, remember, insults are external to us. We cannot control them, but we can ignore them. When you ignore insults, insults are not insults anymore. They are just words.

> What does it mean to be insulted? Stand by a stone and insult it, what response will you get? Likewise, if you listen like a stone, what would the abuser gain from his abuse? However, if you have some weakness, then he has an advantage over you.
>
> Epictetus, *Discourses* 1.25

4. You are taking it too seriously: Deflect it with humor

Insults are designed to hurt us. Insults gain power when we resist them. This is why, when you resist people, they double down on what they say. But when we don't resist them, insults lose their power. This is what happens when we ignore other people's insults. But there is an even better way. We can accept them with humor. We can make them light. As Epictetus once said of someone who insulted him:

> the person obviously didn't know me well enough, or he would have brought up much more damning flaws in my character.
>
> Epictetus, *Discourses*

So lighten up. Don't take insults too seriously. Join the person who insults you. Resistance is the fuel that drives the insult. It is no fun to insult you if you join the person who insults you!

Follow the Stoics and never feel insulted again.

TAKEAWAYS

Insults are not insults unless we choose to be offended by them. Before getting insulted, think of the following:

1. The person may not have meant it as an insult. It just came across that way.

2. What you considered as an insult may not be an insult at all. Maybe it is the truth you need to see.

3. It is an insult only because you treat it as an insult.

4. Deflect the insult with a humorous comment.

TRY THIS SIMPLE EXERCISE

The next time you feel insulted, consider different ways of diffusing it:

- Make a joke of it. It will remove the sting, and the insulter will have no reason to continue.

- See whether there is any truth to the insult. If there is, be thankful to the person for pointing it out. You may do better the next time.

- Consider the possibility that the other person may not have meant it as an insult. Maybe they were careless. Maybe they didn't realize that what they said would offend you.

Say to yourself that it is just someone's opinion. You don't have to accept it or be insulted by it.

Avoiding anger

Nine strategies of an emperor

WHY DO WE FEEL ANGRY?

What angers people these days? Almost everything, it seems.

- If someone cuts us off, we get angry.
- If someone ignores us, we get angry.
- If someone cracks a joke at our expense, we get angry.
- If someone bumps into us, we get angry.

It doesn't even need to involve us directly. If someone does something we don't like or if something does not meet our expectations, we get angry.

- If someone wears skimpy clothes, we get angry.
- If someone has different political beliefs, we get angry.
- If someone has different religious beliefs, we get angry.
- If our coffee is cold, we get angry.
- If someone refuses to help the poor even though they can afford it, we get angry.

Stoking anger is a lucrative business. It's a multibillion dollar industry. There is no shortage of TV and radio personalities, social media influencers, and blog writers who manufacture reasons for us to be offended by things that have never offended us before. The more offended we are, the more we listen to them. The more we listen to them, the more money they make.

If we have so many things to be offended by, no wonder we feel weary and bruised by the end of the day. While we don the mantle of victimhood, the person who angered us is probably unaware of our misery and having a good time.

Yet we also know people who hardly take offence at anything and go about their business cheerfully. If you point out the offence they were subjected to, they probably will give you a blank stare and steer you into something more upbeat.

What is their secret?

THE EMPEROR'S NINE

Emperor Marcus Aurelius, prone to anger quickly, thought through this problem and devised nine ways to handle those we think have offended us (*Meditations* 8.18). Depending on the situation, you may want to look at it from one or more of these points of view to keep your cool when you face something that offends you.

1. We know better

Higher animals feed on lower animals. Being at the top of the hierarchy, human beings are different. We know better, and we are made for each other. So when you are offended the next time, think about your role as a human being. We are each other's protectors and should be in harmony, not conflict. We should know that anger is not a rational way to solve problems.

Isn't it more pleasant not to get angry and get on with your life?

2. The offender doesn't know any better

The person who offended you is by nature so. If you observe them, you'll see that they exhibit this type of behavior, whether sitting at a dinner table or lying in bed. They are opinionated and arrogant and will act this way no matter who they deal with. They act the way they do, not because of you but because of their nature. When we see this, we will also see that there is no reason for us to be angry with the offender.

Why should you be angry when it has nothing to do with you, except that you happen to be in the way?

3. You may be mistaken

Your partner says that you are insensitive and you are angry. You think that your partner is wrong or being unfair. What if they are right? So consider whether the other person may be right and you are not. If they are right, you should be thanking them and not be offended by them. Maybe it is you who is wrong.

Why be angry when the other person is telling the truth?

4. You have offended others in past

If you are honest with yourself, you'll see you have offended others in the past. We all offend others, sometimes deliberately but often without meaning to. Remember the times when you wanted to offend others and held back only because you were afraid of repercussions?

Why take offence at others behaving just as you do at times?

5. You don't know their motives

We are too quick to take offence and take things personally. The person who cut you off may have swerved to avoid an accident. The person who almost bumped into you may be in a rush to see their friend admitted to a hospital. Your boss who pointed out your mistake may have done so because she wants you to succeed.

Why take offence at an action that is not aimed at offending you at all?

6. Life is too short to spend on grievance

Our lives will be over altogether too soon. You must decide whether to spend yours in anger or good cheer.

Why spend the precious little time we are given on this earth being angry rather than letting go?

7. It is your thought that angers you

We spend much time reviewing the offence that someone inflicted on us. We replay, exaggerate, and colorize the offence. All this is happening in our minds. We are writing the script and directing the movie. We are angry by our portrayal of the offence rather than by what happened.

Why be angry when it is in your power not to be?

8. You are adding fuel to the fire

Someone insults you. That may be bad. But when you get angry and upset, you are feeding your suffering. This feeding of anger and upset creates more suffering than the insult itself. You are adding fuel to the fire.

Why add to your suffering when you don't have to?

9. Why not try kindness?

You can choose to be kind even to the most abusive person in the world. If your kindness is genuine, it will diffuse the offence. If they are not challenged, the offender might even be willing to listen to you. Then you can explain your point of view to them. In any case, it will make you less agitated and more rational.

Why not see things from the other person's point of view and correct misperceptions rather than be angry?

And here is an additional suggestion. An emperor's bonus, if you will.

10. It's absurd to expect bad people not to do wrong

Suppose that the other person is bad and hurt you deliberately. Why do you expect bad people not to offend you? You know such people offend others, so why should you be an exception?

Why expect bad people to be good to you?

TAKEAWAYS

We can avoid anger if we follow these nine (plus one) principles:

1. You know better.
2. The offender doesn't know any better.
3. You may be mistaken.
4. You have offended others in the past.
5. You don't know the offender's motives.
6. Life is too short to spend on grievances.
7. It's your thoughts that are offending you.
8. Your thoughts add fuel to the fire.
9. You can try kindness.
10. It is absurd to expect others not to offend you.

TRY THIS SIMPLE EXERCISE

The next time you feel angry, go through these ten suggestions and see how to apply one or more of them to your situation. If you practice often enough, you'll be less and less offended by people and situations.

Getting rid of guilt

How to avoid unnecessary feelings of guilt

WHAT IS GUILT?

How strange is this? We are the accuser, we are the accused, we are the judge, and we are the jury. We punish ourselves for something we did or did not do. No proof is needed. It may be for something that happened 2 minutes ago, 20 years ago, or never. No statute of limitations. It may be for the harm you have caused yourself or someone else. You don't even have to know. The offence may be small (you said something slightly negative about a friend when she is not around) or big (you may have caused serious physical harm to someone).

Yes, this is guilt. People use it as a weapon against us, and we use it as a weapon against others. In many cultures, guilt is deliberately induced in children and others so they will conform to social, cultural, and religious norms. When we grow up, we internalize this and admonish ourselves for whatever we think we shouldn't have done and feel guilty. It is a way of punishing ourselves. Sometimes, we may feel guilty about things that we have no direct part in causing, such as social conditions in a poor country.

While guilt may serve some useful purpose as our conscience-keeper, in most instances, it is a relic of past conditioning and may have outlived its usefulness. It lets other people manipulate us. It pulls back from being joyful, even when there's no reason for it.

Here are some reasons why we feel guilty and what to do about them.

1. Guilt over things we did that we weren't supposed to do

One of the most common types of guilt is feeling guilty about something you did that you weren't supposed to. For example, we may do something like lose our temper but almost simultaneously realize that it is the wrong thing to do. We may do things that are advantageous to us but not necessarily to others. From our early childhood, we were taught that we should not lose our temper and we should not be selfish. From time to time, we break these rules and immediately pay for them by feeling guilty.

Assume that the rule you broke is still relevant to you, and you believe that it is not a good idea to break it. Losing your temper because someone is annoying you could be an example. In these cases, you apply "the first rule" of Stoicism: *If something has already happened, it is not under your control now; if something is not under your control, it is nothing to you.* You may resolve not to repeat your behavior in the future, but for what you are feeling guilty about now, you can do nothing. Imagine the same thing happening in the future and practice behaving differently. Feeling guilty is a waste of time. It can only ruin the present without doing anything to change the past.

2. Guilt over things we didn't intend

Sometimes, we do things with good intentions, but it turns out that we are mistaken about what might happen in the future. We feel guilty because the results of what we did are embarrassing. For example, you give generously to a homeless person, only to find that the homeless person is an addict and used your money to buy more drugs. Yet, at the time you made the decision, you did what you thought to be the best. Your intention was not to support the drug habit but to help a homeless person. For a Stoic, what is important is to act virtuously at any given time. It is this virtuous intention and not the results that follow that truly matters. This is not because we don't care but because we realize that we can only do what is under our control (virtuous action). What happens after that is not under our control. There is no point in feeling guilty about it. It's a learning experience, and maybe the next time, we will do better.

> Past and future are both absent; we feel neither of them. But there can be no pain except as the result of what you feel.
>
> Seneca, *Moral Letters* 54

3. Guilt over things that no one cares about

When you break the "rules," the first thing you need to ask yourself is "Is the rule I just broke still relevant?" For example, you didn't follow some rules of etiquette you were taught when you were young. If it turns out that the rule is not relevant, understand that the rule was once relevant and not anymore. You drop the rule along with the guilt that goes with breaking it. We sometimes feel guilty about things others haven't even noticed and, if they had, would not care about. In other words, people feel guilty about things that do not matter to anyone.

Our feelings of guilt can be so strong (especially because of our early conditioning) that, even when we realize that we have not caused any harm or hurt anyone and stop feeling guilty about it, *we feel guilty about not feeling guilty*.

> Souls that enjoy being sick and that seize upon excuses
> for sorrow are saddened by events long past and erased
> from the records.
>
> Seneca, *Moral Letters* 54

The virtue of justice

When you think you have done something wrong, usually, the virtue you neglected to observe is the virtue of justice. You were perhaps unfair to someone. Going forward, you may want to be more conscious of this. Do all in your power to repair what you have neglected to do or undo the harm you might have caused others. It is much more productive to follow virtue than to feel guilty for not following it.

TAKEAWAYS

1. We feel guilty when we believe we have done something that we shouldn't have done. We become our own accuser—we judge that we were wrong, and we punish ourselves by feeling guilty.

2. Feeling guilty is often meaningless because:

   a. It is possible the thing you feel guilty about may be nothing to feel guilty about.

b. Even if you have done something wrong, you cannot go back and fix the past. So, there is no point in feeling guilty.

c. You might not have intended to do what you did. If your intentions were good, what you did was the best you could. So why feel guilty about it?

d. If you have done something wrong, the best way to deal with it is to acknowledge it, mend the situation if possible, and resolve to act better in the future. Feeling guilty does not help anyone.

TRY THIS SIMPLE EXERCISE

Take five minutes and list all the things, big and small, you feel guilty about.

Look at the first one.

1. Did you intend to do this even though it turned out to be wrong? If the answer is no, then there is no point in feeling guilty about it. You cannot apply your current knowledge to past situations.

2. Is it an insignificant thing that no one is really bothered by? If yes, why feel guilty about something no one cares about?

3. Is it something that you can make amends for now? If yes, make amends, and you will have no reason to feel guilty.

4. Is it something that you can do nothing about now? Simply resolve not to repeat such behavior in the future.

Repeat the procedure one by one to the other things you feel guilty about.

Antidotes to anxiety

How to be anxiety-free

OUR ANXIOUS LIVES

What are we anxious about? Almost everything. Am I over-weight? Am I eating processed foods too much? Am I exercising enough? Am I saving enough for my retirement? Will AI take my job? Am I going to be late for work? What if I fall ill? What if my partner leaves me? What if my new boss doesn't like me? The list is endless, and you can add a hundred things I haven't even thought of to it.

And that's not all. Even in moments of calm, a low hum of anxiety permeates our existence like an ever-present soundtrack. We are never 100 percent there, anywhere. We are never comfortable being where we are. We think about work when we are at play and think about play when we are at work. Anxiety is the most commonly diagnosed mental health condition in the United States. And yet, we know that true happiness cannot be achieved unless we get rid of our anxiety.

> True happiness is [...] to enjoy the present without anxious dependence upon the future.
>
> Seneca, *On Benefits* 7.2

What can we do about it? Here are some antidotes to anxiety that you may find helpful.

Antidote 1: Most fears are imaginary

We are anxious about the future. What if I fall seriously ill? What if I don't have enough money saved for the future? What if the cyst the doctor found in my body turns out to be malignant? What if I make a fool of myself in the job interview? What if I lose my job? What if my spouse finds someone more attractive? What if my investments fail? These things are not happening in the present, but you fear they may happen in the future. You may even imagine that they *will* happen in the future. So you start getting anxious, anticipating the worst. If something bad can happen, we tend to assume that it *will* happen. But many things we assume may never come to pass.

> I am an old man and have known a great many troubles,
> most of which never happened.
>
> Mark Twain

Yes, our life is full of troubles that never happen.

> We are more often frightened than hurt; and we suffer
> more from imagination than from reality.
>
> Seneca, *Moral Letters* 13

Most of our anxieties will never come to pass. Why be anxious?

Antidote 2: Being anxious doesn't help

"Ah," you may say, "but I *know* it is sure to happen." And you may explain why you know for sure something is going to happen. You have no reason to be anxious, even when your fears are not imaginary. If you know that something will happen for sure, you only have two options open to you. The first one is you can do nothing about it. If you can do nothing, why worry about it? Why not wait until it happens and then see how best to respond? Anxiety will not improve your problem-solving skills. The second one is you can do something about it. Think more clearly about this and do what you can now to forestall what you think will happen or minimize its negative effects if it does happen. Once you have done this, you have nothing more to be anxious about. Being anxious about something that has not yet happened adds to your suffering.

> He suffers more than necessary, who suffers before it is necessary.
>
> Seneca, *Moral Letters* 98

Antidote 3: You will have resources available to you in the future

When we believe we have to be anxious about the future *now*, we tell ourselves that we will be helpless in the future. Yet, throughout your life, you have faced many problems and solved them. Why do you assume you won't be able to do the same in the future? What has guided you through thus far will guide you in the future. The mental resources you have now will also be available to you in the future.

> Never let the future disturb you. You will meet it, if you
> have to, with the same weapons of reason which today
> arm you against the present.
>
> Marcus Aurelius, *Meditations* 7.8

It is important to keep our rational faculties intact. They will guide us when we face difficult situations in the future. There is no need to be miserable now, anticipating things going wrong.

Antidote 4: No need to have FOMO on sorrow

People have a fear of missing out (FOMO). It is a feeling that we have to do something right now; otherwise, we will miss something important. A few examples:

You hear about a hot new stock that everyone is investing in, and you might be tempted to invest hastily without doing proper research.

Your friends are talking about the latest gadgets or apps, and you end up purchasing something so you are not missing out on the experience.

When you see your friends posting pictures from a party or event you weren't invited to, you start feeling anxious about missing out on their fun.

FOMO may not be a great way to run your life, but at least it makes sense if you feel you are missing out on good things if you don't take action.

But, when you are anxious, you suffer before the event is yet to happen (if it happens at all). It is like saying, "What I am anxious about may never happen. But I don't want to miss out on the experience of being miserable. Let me start being unhappy right now." After all, who wants to miss out on misery? Seneca has something to say on this:

> What need is there to take an advance on future troubles, ruining the present with fear of the future? When troubles come, it is time enough to bear them. Surely, it is foolish to be miserable now just because you are going to be miserable later on!
>
> Seneca, *Moral Letters* 24

BEING ANXIETY-FREE

How do we get rid of worries about the future? You may rightly argue that you *should* be concerned about the future. You may not save enough if you are not concerned about your old age. If you are not concerned about being late, you may not get to your meeting on time. Yes, we need to be *concerned* about what will happen in the future, but we don't have to be anxious about it. The most important thing we can do to avoid anxiety is first to identify what is and what is not *under our control. Then, take action on what is under your control and deal with what is not under your control as and when it happens.*

Once you have done that, if you still feel anxious, know that your anxiety is likely imaginary, and being anxious doesn't help, and you will have resources available when undesirable things happen in the future. It is absurd to be unhappy now because you *may* be unhappy in the future.

If you are still anxious, Epictetus has a couple of questions for you:

> You now know the principles. You claim to understand them. Then why aren't you putting these principles into practice? What kind of teacher are you waiting for?
>
> Epictetus, *Encheirdion* 51

The present moment exists for us to "enjoy the festival of life," as Epictetus called it. To make the best use of it, we need to eliminate our anxieties about our future. Once we realize that we have done all that we can about the future and there is nothing we can do about it, there is only one thing left: Enjoy the present.

TAKEAWAYS

We fail to enjoy our lives when we are anxious. But most of our anxieties serve no purpose. We can get rid of most of our anxieties if we realize:

1. Most of our anxieties are imaginary. They never come to pass.
2. Anxiety consumes the present without providing for the future. So it is useless.
3. We underestimate our ability to cope with any situation that may arise in the future.
4. What we are anxious about may or may not happen. So why be anxious about something that may never happen?
5. The best way to deal with anxiety is to do what we can now and wait for the future to arrive.

TRY THIS SIMPLE EXERCISE

Think about all the things that you are anxious about. Write them down.

For each one, ask these questions:

- How sure are you that it is likely to happen? If you think that it is unlikely, why waste time being anxious about it now?

- What can you do about it now? If you can do something about it, do it. If you cannot, then why be anxious about it? You can deal with it if it ever happens.

- You have faced many situations in the past and are still standing. Why will this thing you are anxious about defeat you? Remember, you will have the same resources to live well as you had all your life.

Overcoming helplessness

How to avoid the feeling of helplessness

THE FEELING OF HELPLESSNESS

Why do we get angry? Because someone said or did something that we thought was offensive? Why are we afraid? Because we are anxious about the future? Why do we subject ourselves to any negative emotion? Because something or someone upset us?

It doesn't matter why we are angry, afraid, or upset. We just feel that the situations and the people we face are difficult to deal with. We lack the confidence to find a rational solution. We know this to be true because we have seen people remain calm under aggravating conditions. They are confident that they can deal with hostile conditions. We lack similar confidence, and we attribute our lack of confidence to something outside of us: other people and our circumstances. But the reality is just the opposite. It is our inner lack of confidence that has created the outer difficulties with people and circumstances.

> Our lack of confidence doesn't come from difficulty; the difficulty comes from our lack of confidence.
>
> Seneca, *Moral Letters* 21

We get angry, upset, or depressed because we look at our problems and feel we are too impotent to face them. We feel helpless. We lash out against anything that we think is the source of our problem. Our negativity is often tied to our helplessness.

WE OVERLOOK THE RESOURCES WE HAVE

But we are NOT helpless. We have tremendous resources within us that we habitually fail to use. We are provided with resources to face every challenge we come across. Suppose someone says something negative about you. The first impulse may be to be angry with that person. But then you have the resource of patience, which you can use to choose not to be angry. You are at a gym, working out. You find it hard and feel like giving up. But you have the resources of endurance to keep going.

In fact, whenever you face a difficult situation, your first impulse is to give in to some negative emotion because of your (most likely) learned helplessness. So the next time you are about to give in to a negative emotion, ask yourself, "Do I have any resources within me that I can use without giving in too easily to this negative emotion?" You may be surprised to find that you have the resources to deal with the situation, and yet you are prematurely giving in.

> Remember that for every challenge you face, you have the resources within you to cope with that challenge. If you are inappropriately attracted to someone, you will find you have the resource of self-restraint. When you have pain, you have the resource of endurance. When you are insulted, you have the resource of patience. If you start thinking along these lines, you will soon find

that you don't have a single challenge for which you
don't have the resources to cope.

Epictetus, *Encheiridion* 9

TAKEAWAYS

1. We get angry or upset when we feel helpless.
2. But we always have resources to cope with any situation.
3. So, we should look for resources we have to handle any problem that arises rather than feel helpless about it.

TRY THIS EXERCISE

Here is an exercise to train yourself in finding the resources you have:

1. Take a sheet of paper. Divide it into four columns.
2. In the first column, think of all the negative emotions you feel frequently.
3. In the second column, choose an example for each negative emotion.
4. In the third column, think of an internal resource you can use instead of giving in to the negative emotion.
5. In the fourth column, write down how the situation could have turned out differently if you had used that resource.

You can repeat this exercise many times and on different days, so the next time a negative emotion comes up, your first reaction will not be to give in but to examine what resources are available to you and use them.

As you repeat this exercise, you may be pleasantly surprised to know that you have more resources than you realize.

You don't need their approval

How to be independent of other people's opinions

WE CRAVE APPROVAL

Are we worried about whether others will approve of us? "Of course not!" we may protest. But a moment's reflection will tell us how much of what we want in life—the car we want to drive, the house we want to live in, the neighborhood we want to move into, the reputation we wish to achieve, and a hundred other things—is influenced by our need to be approved by others. Think about people buying new clothes when they go on a vacation. They are trying to seek the approval of those they have never met and those they will never meet again. Ridiculous as this may sound, sometimes we are more concerned about being respected by people we don't even respect. It is comical that we want the approval of even those we despise—sometimes, especially those we despise!

> Who are these people that you want to be admired by?
> Aren't they the same ones whom you used to call crazy?
> Well, then, do you want to be admired by madmen?
>
> Epictetus, *Discourses* 1.21

Yet, it is not a harmless pursuit. A vast part of our anxiety can be traced back to our preoccupation with what others think. Such is the need for the approval of others.

You may ask what's wrong with seeking the approval of others. We live in a society, and isn't it better to be approved rather than be disapproved by others? Shouldn't we seek the approval of our teachers, parents, and others who try to guide us on the right path? Yes, there is nothing wrong with seeking someone's approval if you think that they are leading you to excellence. But mostly, we seek approval of our behavior that has nothing to do with excellence. It's just someone else's opinion. Their opinion is no more valid than yours.

SEEKING APPROVAL MAKES US SHEEP-LIKE

When we seek approval, we want to be like everyone else. We accept untested advice. But following the masses will not lead us to a principled and happy life.

> Nothing gets us into greater trouble than our belief in untested advice, our habit of thinking that what others think as good must be good, believing counterfeits as being truly good, and living our life not by reason but by imitating others.
>
> Seneca, *On Happiness* 1

SO, WHAT CAN WE DO?

Whenever we are bothered by what others think, we can remind ourselves of the Stoic principles and ask ourselves a few questions:

- Do we want to do what we believe to be right or what someone else thinks we should do?

- When we are doing the right thing, why should other people's opinions matter?

- Are we sure that other people are so wise that we should follow them?

- Who lives with the consequences of our actions—us or others?

Most likely, we will notice that we seek the approval of others mostly because of our anxiety, and what we need to do is to live the way we believe to be right and ignore public opinion. And remember the words of Marcus Aurelius:

> Don't waste the rest of your life worrying about others—unless it is for some mutual benefit. The time you spend wondering what so-and-so is doing, saying, thinking, or plotting is the time that's lost for some other task.
>
> Marcus Aurelius, *Meditations* 3.4

Here are four specific suggestions to help you avoid seeking other people's approval rather than walking your own path:

1. Seek freedom rather than seek approval

We can realize enormous freedom right now by doing just one thing—by not worrying about what others think of us. Just by ignoring what others think, we will gain more time and be more tranquil. To achieve a good life, we need to conform to what is virtuous and not to what others think.

> If you do not worry about what others think, say, or do
> but only about whether your actions are just and godly,
> you will gain time and tranquility. [...] Run straight
> towards your goal without looking left or right.
>
> Marcus Aurelius, *Meditations* 4.18

When your actions are guided by your principles, you don't even have to care if others think what you do is shameful or miserable.

> [The Stoic sage] pays no attention to what others consider
> shameful or miserable. He does not walk with the crowd.
>
> Seneca, *On the Firmness of the Wise Man* 14,3–4

2. Seek to do the right thing rather than seek approval

What others approve of may not be the right thing to do. As Epicurus said:

> "What I know, they do not approve. What they approve,
> I do not know."
>
> Quoted by Seneca, *Moral Letters* 29

What is the payoff for walking the road all by yourself, whether anyone else joins you or not?

3. Seek wisdom rather than seek approval

We all *like* other people's approval. We would rather be applauded than derided. And yet, it should not drive what we do. When we set approval-seeking as the goal, the possibilities of a virtue-based life diminish.

- Are we going to do what is wise or what others approve of?

- Are we going to do what is just or what others approve of?

- Are we going to do what is moderate or what others approve of?

- Are we going to do what is courageous or what others approve of?

As long as we have a life guided by principles (such as Stoicism), seeking approval can only damage the principles and curtail our freedom to act. We will be sacrificing ourselves and our principles for the sake of approval and the unstable opinions of other people. We even care about what a stranger or even someone we don't respect might think of us.

> How foolish one must be to leave a lecture hall gratified by the applause of the ignorant! Why do you take pleasure in praise from those you cannot praise yourself?
>
> Seneca, *Moral Letters* 52

4. Seek to do your best rather than seek approval

The need for approval also makes us susceptible to flattery. Others can manipulate us by shaping our behavior to their liking by approving or disapproving our behavior. As others manipulate us, we gradually move away from principles that guide our lives in the right direction. A Stoic does what is virtuous, whether it brings flattery or disapproval.

> As long as you control your desires and aversions, there is nothing to worry about. This is your opening

statement, your case, and your proof. This is your last
word and your acquittal.

Epictetus, *Discourses* 2.2

As Abraham Lincoln observed when asked about other people's criticism:

I do the very best I know how—the very best I can; and
I mean to keep doing so until the end. If the end brings
me out alright, what is said against me won't amount
to anything. If the end brings me out wrong, ten angels
swearing I was right would make no difference.

Quoted in Fred G. Carpenter, *Six Months at the*
White House with Abraham Lincoln

TAKEAWAYS

We crave the approval of others. But when we do what is right,
other people's opinions do not matter. Instead of seeking approval:

1. Seek freedom.
2. Seek to do the right things.
3. Seek wisdom.
4. Seek to do your best.

When you are free, when you do what is right and wise, and
when you do your best, you don't need anyone's approval.

TRY THIS EXERCISE

Whenever you are bothered by other people's opinions, examine what you are being criticized for. Now ask yourself:

- Is your action wise and not foolish?
- Is it fair to others and not unjust?
- Is it moderate and not excessive?
- Is it courageous and not cowardly?

If you can answer yes to all questions, you can safely ignore other people's opinions. If you answer no to any of the questions above, maybe you should correct yourself.

Facing adversity

How to be resilient

We all face adversity, some of us more often than others. The cause could be someone we know, someone we don't know, or some condition in our life we need to face: insults, isolation, illness, loss of material things or loved ones, poverty, betrayal, heartbreak, natural disasters, and so on. The list can be long, especially for those who are not resilient. Most of us are not good at facing adversity. We would rather be safe in our own world than face the difficulties that get in our way. And yet adversity often helps us move forward. We emerge stronger when facing and handling it. Adversity is the wind that propels the sailboat forward. Here are some suggestions for handling adversity:

1. Adversity has a short shelf-life

In general, adversity is short-lived. We tend to prolong it by plotting our counterattack, brooding about it, getting angry, and so on. Our prolonging makes adversity a lot worse than it is. In life, adversity and good fortune alternate, which means that we can expect our conditions to change for the better.

> In the day of prosperity, let no one be overjoyed. In
> the day of adversity, let no one faint; the successions of
> fortune alternate.
>
> Seneca, *Natural Questions* 3, Preface

It is less difficult to endure adversity when you know it is temporary and better times may be ahead.

2. Adversity is not personal

We tend to treat every misfortune and adversity that comes our way as personal. We ask, "Why me?" Yet, we know that when our flight is cancelled, it is not personal. When a cyclone destroys your home, it is not personal. Even when someone deliberately gets in your way, it is not personal. Given their genetics and upbringing, they acted in the only way they could have. There is a long chain of causality, and they are just a link in the chain. So when you face adversity, remember this: It is not personal. Things unfold as links in a long causal chain.

> Has anything happened to you? Good. It's supposed
> to happen.
>
> Marcus Aurelius, *Meditations* 4.26

Most things are impersonal, and things are not as bad as they seem. The person who just insulted you may be going through a rough patch in their life. You just happened to be the object available to them against which they expressed their frustration. You are not the target. If somebody else were in your place, they would have been subjected to the same insult.

3. Adversity can be turned to your advantage

If you want to excel in any sport, you want to train with the best. For example, if you are a wrestler, you want to practice with the best wrestler. This gives you the best opportunity to not only maintain your current levels of fitness and expertise but also increase them. Weak opponents cannot be of much help.

> Each needs someone with whom one may make comparisons and investigations. Skilled wrestlers are kept up to the mark by practice.
>
> Seneca, *Moral Letters* 109

Adversity is like a wrestler, and strong adversity is like a strong wrestler. You can view the great adversities you face as wrestlers you were sent to practice with so you can increase your resilience. Seneca even suggests that:

> Fortune offers us opportunities […] We ought to move and not to become frozen and still by fear. Nay, he is the best man who, through peril, menaces him on every side and arms and chains beset his path, nevertheless neither impairs not conceals his virtue; for to keep oneself safe does not mean to bury oneself.
>
> Seneca, *On the Tranquility of Mind* 5

Adversity provides an opportunity to practice our goodness and to be a better person. It gives an opportunity to practice kindness or wisdom. Good cannot exist without bad. You can counterbalance what you see as bad with what you consider good. A situation will not look as bad if some good comes out of it.

Also, remember that, once you go through adversity, you are better off. The greater the adversity, the greater the gain when you go through it and come out unscathed.

> What does not kill me makes me stronger.
>
> Friedrich Nietzsche, *Twilight of the Idols*

4. Adversity is not intrinsically "bad"

Adversities are external to us, and therefore, they are indifferents, neither good nor bad. Since they are not in our control, we should deal with them as they present themselves. They are bound to happen in the course of one's life. Since indifferents are not essential for our happiness, we put them in perspective and examine what appropriate action we can take that would be compatible with virtue. We act accordingly.

> You have seen all that [adversity]. Now look at this. Your part is to be serene, to be simple […] Life is short. Get as much as you can from each passing hour.
>
> Marcus Aurelius, *Meditations* 4.26

The next time you face adversity, remember it is not personal. It is temporary. See it as something designed to let you practice your resilience. Your job is to be serene and simple in the face of adversity and get the most out of your life in spite of the adversity you face.

When you see that adversity is temporary and impersonal, that there is nothing "bad" about it, and that it can be turned to your advantage, you will be less bothered by it.

TAKEAWAYS

When faced with adversity, remember the following:

1. Adversity has a short shelf-life. Whether it is a natural disaster or the enmity of a person, it will pass soon enough. Meanwhile, do without mental agitation.

2. Natural adversity is not personal. Natural disasters, diseases, accidents—all such things happen to everyone.

3. Even personal adversity may not be personal. A person who is belligerent with you may have had a bad day.

4. Treat adversity as an opportunity to practice serenity.

TRY THIS EXERCISE

Cast your mind back, maybe ten years. What adversities did you face? How long did they last? If you cannot remember anything significant, it may be because what seemed to be adversity then passed into nothingness as time went by.

If you can remember something significant, ask yourself whether it was such a major disaster as it seemed to you then. Realize that adversities don't last long. They pass.

See that it is best not to give in to adversities because they pass soon enough.

Handling ingratitude

How to cope with ingratitude

It is common for human beings to give and take. We generally expect the other person to reciprocate when we give—maybe not immediately, but sometime in the future. Even if they don't or can't reciprocate, we assume they are thankful for what they have received. But there are people who not only don't reciprocate but don't even acknowledge what you have done for them. They take the benefits they receive for granted and act as if they have nothing to be thankful for.

Such ingratitude bothers many people on the giving end. We cannot understand how someone who has benefited from us can refuse to do even simple things for us when we seek their help. We become strangers to them once they receive whatever they can get from us. It's not just their failure to return favors that annoys us; their indifference roils us. We feel cheated and exploited.

We wonder how to deal with such ingratitude. Do we remind them what we did for them? Do we become angry and upset? Do we ignore those in need? Do we stop doing favors? Do we indirectly hint at their ungrateful behavior?

The Stoic answer is *none of the above*.

1. Why are you surprised?

When you are surprised by someone's ungratefulness, think of this first. Why are you surprised? Why weren't you expecting such behavior? Isn't it obvious that ungrateful people will behave this way? Or, were you expecting everyone you encounter to be a grateful person?

> So what is surprising or wrong about boors behaving
> boorishly? Shouldn't you rather blame yourself for not
> anticipating that they would behave this way? You are a
> rational being and have the means of knowing that it is
> likely that they would behave this way. You forgot, and
> now you are surprised.
>
> Marcus Aurelius, *Meditations* 10.42

So get over your surprise and remember that, under the circumstances, what happened is what you should expect. There is no need to get upset.

2. Do you need a reward for being good?

Why do we do things that benefit others? To be rewarded in return? If so, you are in a business transaction and got a bad deal. However, if you are a practicing Stoic, you don't treat your action as a business deal. You practice four excellences: practical wisdom, courage, restraint, and justice. When you practice the four excellences, your actions flow from your excellence and are not influenced by an expectation of a reward. When you do something for the benefit of others, it is complete in itself.

Remember that we control only our thinking and our actions, not other people's thinking or actions. So, don't expect them to behave a certain way or do something. Don't expect anything from them. It's their job to be grateful. It's futile to complain about how others are. They are what they are and do what they do.

> Once you have done someone a service, what more do you want? Aren't you happy enough that you followed the laws of nature? Are you also expecting to be paid for it? That's like the eye expecting a reward for seeing or the feet for walking. That's what they are made for. They do their part by doing what they were created to do. Similarly, a human being is born to be kind. When you have done something kind or something else for the common good, you have done what you are made for. You get what is your own.
>
> Marcus Aurelius, *Meditations* 10.42

So, know that your reward is your act of kindness and generosity. It is done; it is over. What upsets you now is your own expectation, not someone else's ingratitude.

> You have done a good deed, and someone benefited from it. Why are you, like an idiot, holding out for more—such as applause for your kindness or some favor in return?
>
> Marcus Aurelius, *Meditations* 7.73

3. Do you want to avoid being good?

Because of your frustration with ungrateful people, you may be tempted to become too cautious and stop helping others and giving them gifts. This would be a mistake. As Seneca points out, it's like a farmer refusing to sow again after a poor harvest, a sailor refusing to try the sea ever again after a shipwreck, or a banker refusing to lend again because of his experience with swindlers.

> If one were compelled to drop everything that caused trouble, life would soon grow dull amid sluggish idleness.
>
> Seneca, *Moral Letters* 81

Besides, if you feel that more people are ungrateful than grateful, then it makes sense to help as many people as possible—it would be a pleasure to find people who are grateful, but that's not the reason we act to benefit others.

4. Do you think your good comes from others?

Most importantly, when we expect gratitude from others, our good comes from us and not from others. We are not being helpful or giving gifts to get something back from others. Because our good comes from us and only from us, we are concerned with how we act, not how others may respond. When we do things for the benefit of others, it's because it's an attribute of ours we value. It's not a commercial transaction. There is no balance sheet.

Yes, it would be nice if people were grateful. That may be our "preferred indifferent." But people don't need to be grateful. An ungrateful person cannot control us—they can't make us withdraw, can't make us less charitable, and can't hurt us. The only person they can hurt is themselves.

No matter what we lose or gain in life or how others treat us, we aim to act in a way that is consistent with the excellences we practice. No one can take this away from us by their ingratitude.

After Stilpo's homeland was captured and he lost his wife and children, he emerged happy from his isolation. When Demetrius [...] asked him if he had lost anything, Stilpo replied, "I've all my goods with me!"

Seneca, *Moral Letters* 9

Your goods are always with you and only with you. There is no need to be upset by someone else's ingratitude.

TAKEAWAYS

1. Once we do a generous or kind act, it is complete. There is no reason to expect anything in return.

2. We should not withhold being generous and kind because people are not grateful. It is like a farmer refusing to farm because of a poor harvest.

3. Our good comes from ourselves. Others' lack of gratitude has nothing to do with what we do.

TRY THIS SIMPLE EXERCISE

Did you ever complain to others or to yourself about someone's ingratitude? Ask yourself these questions:

1. Why do you expect a reward for being good? Is being good not enough?

2. Would you want to do fewer good acts because you were not rewarded?

3. Does your good come from yourself or others?

4. Why do you need others to acknowledge your good?

Handling betrayal

How to cope with betrayal

TRUST AND BETRAYAL

One thing that makes our lives pleasant is the sense of trust. We trust our family, friends, coworkers, and others near and dear to us. When you trust someone, you believe they will stand by you, probably forever.

Then something happens. You feel you have been betrayed by someone you trusted. It is one thing if an acquaintance or a stranger has betrayed you; it is quite another if you have been betrayed by someone you knew and trusted. You have that sinking feeling. If the betrayal is serious, you feel the ground under your feet collapse. You are not standing on a solid rock anymore but sinking in quicksand. It is not very pleasant, but there it is.

You can't stop thinking about it. How could they have done this to you? You feel humiliated. Now, your mind goes out of control. It starts finding ways to get back at the person who betrayed you.

But we know this is not the Stoic way. What should we do?

EXAMINE WHETHER YOU GOT IT RIGHT

We often react in predictable ways. When we step on something sharp, we immediately lift our foot, even before we realize we have stepped on something sharp. When someone tells us that we are stupid, we get angry, even before we examine why the other person said that. In fact, over time, most reactions become thoughtless. Our first reactions are driven by instinct, habit, upbringing, or conditioning. They may or may not be appropriate or in our best interests, but we seldom stop to reconsider our first reactions to things. Examining our impressions can go a long way in lightening our suffering. So, let's examine your impression that you have been betrayed.

> Start by challenging everything that appears disagreeable. "You are only an appearance. Let me fully understand what you are."
>
> Epictetus, *Encheiridion* 1

MAYBE IT IS YOU WHO BETRAYED THEM

Have you considered that you may have been betrayed because the other person thought you betrayed them first? Before becoming defensive about this, consider the possibility that we do things that may seem harmless to us, but others may not see it that way. Any family counsellor would tell you that family members accuse each other of betraying them. The person acted the way they did because of their impression of behavior, even if that impression is incorrect. This means they did not betray you as you thought they did. They repaid you in the way they thought you treated them.

MAYBE YOU MISUNDERSTOOD

The friend you thought betrayed you by refusing to help you may have their own more serious problems to cope with. Your business associate who refused to lie to the boss to save your job may not have betrayed you but did what he thought was right.

So, whenever you think someone has betrayed you, examine it to see if it is true. See it from the other person's perspective. In many cases, you will see that the person, for the most part, is not motivated to betray you but to do what is right for them or everyone in general. When you see this, you will see that there is no betrayal. Even if there is, it may not have been as serious as you imagined. There might be many mitigating factors leading up to the other person's actions.

1. There's no reason to feel humiliated

When someone betrays us, we feel humiliated. But we are mistaken. A person betrays another person because of their lack of character. It has nothing to do with us; the shame is not on us. Others do what they do for their reasons. You happen to be at the receiving end of someone else's action. If it were not you, it would have been someone else. People do what they do depending on their nature. Others' actions cannot diminish us. They cannot stop us from leading a life under our control. The only betrayal that should matter to us is the one that comes from us. Others' betrayals are their business. If you are disturbed by other people's betrayals, you may want to think about this:

> How is it that uninformed and ignorant minds confuse
> the informed and trained person?
>
> Marcus Aurelius, *Meditations* 5.32

If we, with our understanding of Stoic principles, cannot see that betrayals are nothing to us and feel humiliated, why should we expect the other person with no training to see the harm in them? Betrayals are not harmful to us but only to the perpetrator.

2. People do things in line with their character

The way we are born and grow up, we develop certain character traits. People who betray us may not have set out to betray us but may have acted in a way "that seemed right to them" (Epictetus). Even if we say that the other person's character is flawed,

> What else could they do—with their character? [...]
> Expecting a bad person not to harm others is like
> expecting a fig tree not to produce fig juice, babies not
> to cry, horses never to neigh, and the other inevitable
> things not to happen.
>
> Marcus Aurelius, *Meditations* 12.16

3. Others' betrayals cannot hurt us

We appoint others as the source of our happiness. When we do this, we will always be at their mercy. But yet, we know that, eventually, our happiness can come only from us. It is natural to be upset if someone betrays us. But if we continue to feel betrayed and if we let it overcome us, we may want to think about this:

> When you blame others for your negative feelings, you
> are being ignorant. When you blame yourself for your
> negative feelings, you are making progress. You are being
> wise when you stop blaming yourself or others.
>
> Epictetus, *Encheiridion* 5

Still can't get over it? If you still hold a grudge after understanding all this, there is only one thing you can do

If you're still angry, then get to work on that.

Marcus Aurelius, *Meditations* 12.16

TAKEAWAYS

Sometimes we feel betrayed; sometimes we are betrayed. When this happens, remember:

1. There is no reason to feel humiliated. People betray us because of their lack of character, which has nothing to do with us.
2. There is no reason to be angry at them, because they think what they did was right. If they are mistaken, we have no reason to be angry.
3. Others' betrayals cannot hurt us because other people are not the source of our happiness. We are.

TRY THIS SIMPLE EXERCISE

Think of a time you felt betrayed by someone close to you. What were your reactions?

- Did you feel humiliated, or did you think it had nothing to do with you and they were just doing what was in line with their character?
- Did you think what they did hurt you, or did you think what others do is external to you and therefore can't hurt you?
- Were you angry at them, or did you think they did not know any better, so there was no need to get angry?

If your answer in each case is the second one, you are on the right path already. If not, the next time you feel betrayed, try to see it from a different perspective.

Getting up every time we fall

How to always land on our feet

Life knocks us down from time to time. We can run away from it, but the problem with avoiding adversity by running away from it is that you may face a different type of trouble. Even if you don't, your world will start shrinking. There are those who, when knocked down, stay down. The resilient get up every time they are knocked down.

> Our greatest glory is not in never falling, but in rising every time we fall.
>
> Confucius, *The Analects*

Stoics did not invite trouble, but they were ready to deal with it if it arrived uninvited.

1. Don't look for an escape hatch—there is none

Many of us believe that we are not resilient enough to bounce back when subjected to adversity. We constantly anticipate adverse conditions, try to hide from trouble, and even run away.

However, there are two problems with this run-and-hide approach. One, no place in the world is 100 percent "safe."

If you escape one type of trouble, you will face another. Two, wherever you go, you take yourself with you. We are the major source of our problems. Even if you leave all your problems behind and move to a new place, your mind will soon create other problems for you.

> Why do you think that running away will help? That which you are running away from is with you at all times. You have to lay aside the load on your mind; until you do this, no place will satisfy you.
>
> Seneca, *Moral Letters* 28

Let's assume that problems and adversity are a part of life. We cannot avoid them because they are outside our control.

> A healthy mind should be ready for whatever may come to pass.
>
> *Marcus Aurelius, Meditations* 10.15

Let's not waste our time looking for an escape hatch. Instead, let's use that energy to find resilience in ourselves when problems knock us down.

2. Prevent problems before they arise—use Hanlon's razor

We tend to attribute motives to people. When someone ignores us, we think the person is arrogant. If the boss disagrees with our suggestion, we think she doesn't like us. We add our interpretation to things, and it is this interpretation that knocks us down. Many of us are not resilient enough to let it go and, instead, brood over it for hours or days. One way to be resilient is to see things as they are without trying to interpret them. Here is Epictetus speaking:

> "His son is dead." "What happened?" "His son is dead."
> "Nothing more?" Nothing more."
> "The ship is lost." "What happened?" "The ship is lost."
> "He was taken to prison." "What happened?" "He was taken to prison."
> "It is too bad for him" is a comment we add on our own.
>
> Epictetus, *Discourses* 3.8

So, someone ignored us—they ignored us—nothing more. We add our own comment that this person is arrogant. When the boss disagreed with us, she disagreed with us—nothing more. She doesn't like us is a comment we add. Our interpretation of events creates much of the adversity we face. We attribute malice to others and even to nature. If we can eliminate our interpretation, we will eliminate much of the adversity and, along with it, things to be resilient against.

Hanlon's razor

How do we do this? One way is to view everything that happens without adding commentary.

> We don't mark him down as bad, we don't take offence, we don't suspect him of plotting against us.
>
> Marcus Aurelius, *Meditations* 6.20

I often use "Hanlon's razor" to eliminate adversarial thoughts.

Never attribute to malice that which is adequately
explained by stupidity.

Napoleon

Originally attributed to Napoleon, this principle is often called
Hanlon's razor. We don't need to think that the other person is
stupid, but we should realize people do things that hurt us even
though they don't feel any malice toward us.

We will not face many mental adversities if we don't attribute
malice (such as arrogance or dislike) to others. We don't need
to worry about resilience when there is no adversity. We don't
need to get up if we don't set ourselves up for a fall.

3. We are more resilient than we think—have that confidence

We are more resilient than we think. Our fear that we won't
be resilient enough when facing problems is a form of learned
helplessness. Most of us fear cancer, and yet, when people get
cancer, they face it with courage.

James Stockdale and John McCain spent several years as pris-
oners of war enduring many hardships. Yet it is doubtful if
they would have thought they could endure torture for several
years. When we anticipate problems, our imagination tells us
we are not strong enough to face difficulties or resilient enough
to bounce back.

We suffer more often in imagination than in reality.

Seneca, *Moral Letters* 13

When we find ourselves in difficult situations, we find resources within ourselves to cope with them—resources we didn't know existed within us.

> Nothing happens to anyone that he is not formed by
> nature to bear.
>
> Marcus Aurelius, *Meditations* 5.18

4. Difficulties build our resilience "muscles" — work them

There is another reason not to be afraid of problems. When we face and overcome a problem—as we usually do—we become more resilient. The more problems we face, the more resilient we become. Fewer and fewer problems knock us down as we strengthen our resilience muscles.

> Difficulties strengthen the mind, as labor does the body.
>
> *Seneca, On Providence*

If all we face is good fortune, we will become powerless to resist adversity.

> Unimpaired good fortune cannot withstand a single blow.
>
> Seneca, *Moral Letters* 57

This does not mean you should deliberately look for problems to build your resilience muscles. Rather, you should try to avoid problems but not run away in fear.

> "In your view, a brave man will expose himself to dangers."
> Not at all. He will not fear them, and he will avoid
> them. Caution suits him, not fear.
>
> Seneca, *Moral Letters* 85

Muscles that are not stressed will lose their strength. If your mind is not stressed, so will your capacity to rebound and be resilient.

TAKEAWAYS

1. Problems are a part of life. We cannot be fearful of them.
2. Running away from problems is a futile exercise.
3. We can prevent problems from arising by not attributing motives to others.
4. We are more resilient than we think.
5. Facing adversity makes us stronger and more resilient.

TRY THIS SIMPLE EXERCISE

Imagine your worst fear. Imagine that it has already happened. Are you knocked down by it? Since it has already happened, it is too late to stop it.

Think about what you can do using the resources you have. Are you so helpless that you can't do anything?

Fast-forward ten years. Where is the problem now?

Final thoughts

Let's not be fooled by simplicity

In this book, we have covered some of the most profound principles that govern our lives. They are easy to understand and simple to practice. Yet they are so effective that they appealed to an emperor and a slave two thousand years ago. They are so profound as to form the basis of some powerful modern psychotherapies.

We have covered some of the basic principles of this incredibly effective philosophy. We have seen what stands in our way of practicing them and how to deal with these obstacles. We have discussed how we can use these principles to design a life that flows well. Finally, we have seen how the principles can be applied to our everyday problems and concerns.

Applying these principles to your life can be done at any time. You can use these principles to design a life that flows smoothly and well. You can also pick any principle that appeals to you and use it to solve a specific problem. But you will get a lot more out of these principles if you use them to design a better life than if you use them randomly.

My wish is that these principles, which were discovered more than two thousand years ago, will make your life richer and make it flow better. I hope you are not fooled by the simplicity of these principles into thinking that the key to the good life cannot be that simple or that obvious. It is.

Thank you for letting me share these principles with you. I wish you well.

Chuck Chakrapani

REFERENCES

Quotes and sources

All Stoic quotes used in this book are referenced in the text. A vast majority of the quotes are taken from the following books:

Chakrapani, Chuck. *Stoic Foundations* (Epictetus' *Discourses* 1, Plain English version), The Stoic Gym, 2017

Chakrapani, Chuck. *Stoic Choices* (Epictetus' *Discourses* 2, Plain English version), The Stoic Gym, 2017

Chakrapani, Chuck. *Stoic Training* (Epictetus' *Discourses* 3, Plain English version), The Stoic Gym, 2018

Chakrapani, Chuck. *Stoic Freedom* (Epictetus' *Discourses* 4, Plain English version), The Stoic Gym, 2018

Chakrapani, Chuck. *The Good Life Handbook* (Epictetus' *Encheiridion*, Plain English version), The Stoic Gym, 2016

Chakrapani, Chuck. *Stoic Meditations* (Marcus Aurelius' *Meditations*, Plain English version), The Stoic Gym, 2018

Chakrapani, Chuck. *Stoic Lessons* (Musonius Rufus' *Lectures* 1, Plain English version), The Stoic Gym, 2018

In addition, I have occasionally used the following sources:

Marcus Aurelius, *Meditations* (Tr. Gregory Hayes), Modern Library, 2003

Marcus Aurelius, *Meditations* (Tr. Robin Warfield), Basic Books, 2021

Epictetus, *Discourses and Selected Writings* (Tr. Robert Dobbin), 2008

Epictetus, *Discourses, Fragment, Handbook* (Tr. Robin Hard), Oxford World Classics, 2014

Seneca, *Letters on Ethics: To Lucilius* (Tr. Margaret Graver and A.A. Long, The University of Chicago Press, 2015

All other Stoic quotes are in the public domain.

GRATITUDE

For those who made this book happen

For almost a decade, I have been writing about Stoicism with a single purpose: to make Stoic ideas accessible to the modern audience, even to those only marginally interested in Stoicism. Much of the material in this book has appeared in some form elsewhere, particularly in *The Stoic Gym's Prokopton Letter*. Over time, several readers expressed interest in having my popular articles gathered in one place, logically organized and formatted. I was actively seeking a compatible publisher to bring this idea to life.

It was then that my good friend Tim LeBon introduced me to Iain Campbell, setting everything in motion. My first thanks, therefore, go to Tim.

Iain Campbell, Publishing Director at Hachette UK, was so enthusiastic about this book that it was an absolute pleasure to work with him. He was receptive to my ideas and brought this book to fruition in a matter of months. We were completely aligned in our vision for the book. Thank you, Iain.

I must also thank this book's copy editor, Antonia Maxwell, for her meticulous attention to detail and for correcting my oversights. My gratitude to you, Antonia.

There are two other individuals—my partner, Nancy Kramarich, and my long-term assistant, Chris Mole—who manage most aspects of my heavily outsourced life. This allows me to focus on the things I truly love, such as writing this book. My deepest thanks to them both.

Over the years, many Stoic scholars, such as A. A. Long, Christopher Gill, and John Sellars, have generously offered their time whenever I needed clarification on Stoic ideas. Prominent modern Stoics, including Donald Robertson, Massimo Pigliucci, and Kai Whiting, have significantly contributed to the growth of *The Stoic*, *The Stoic Gym*, and the Prokopton communities. Thank you all for your invaluable help.

Finally, I thank the Prokopton community, the raison d'être of this book.